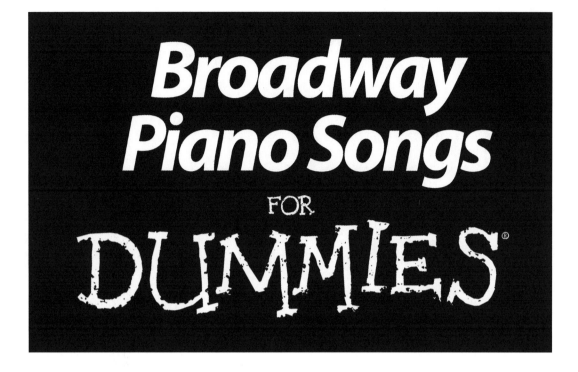

Broadway Piano Songs FOR DUMMIES®

Performance Notes by Adam Perlmutter

ISBN 978-1-4234-2338-6

HAL•LEONARD® CORPORATION

7777 W. BLUEMOUND RD. P.O. BOX 13819 MILWAUKEE, WI 53213

Visit Hal Leonard Online at
www.halleonard.com

Table of Contents

Introduction

•••

*W*elcome to *Broadway Piano Songs For Dummies!* In this book, you can find everything you need to play some of Broadway's most beloved tunes. These great songs span the history of Broadway, from "Ol' Man River" *(Show Boat)* and "My Romance" *(Jumbo)* to "Popular" *(Wicked)* and "Always Look on the Bright Side of Life" *(Spamalot)*. The songs provide glimpses into the work of some of the Great White Way's most revered composers, including Rodgers & Hammerstein, Andrew Lloyd Webber, Cole Porter, and Stephen Schwartz.

About This Book

The music in this book is in standard piano notation — a staff for the melody and lyrics above the traditional piano grand staff. Above the staff, you find the basic chords, along with guitar frames. I assume you know a little something about reading music, and that you know a little bit about playing piano — such as how to hold your fingers, basic chords, and how to look cool while doing it. If you need a refresher course on piano, please check out *Piano For Dummies* by Blake Neely (Wiley).

How to Use This Book

For every song here, I include a brief intro with a little background on the history of the song and the show it comes from. Sometimes I discuss a performer, a composer, or some other, often trivial or otherwise interesting, element of the song. Then I go over a handful of essential tidbits you need as you discover how to play these songs on the piano:

✔ A run-down of the parts you need to know.

✔ A breakdown of some of the chord progressions important to playing the song effectively.

✔ Some of the critical information you need to navigate the sheet music.

✔ Some tips and shortcuts you can use to expedite the learning process.

In many cases, you may already know how to do some of the things that I suggest. If so, please feel free to skip over those familiar bits.

I recommend that you first play through the song, and then practice all the main sections and chords. From there, you can add the tricks and treats of each song — and these classic Broadway songs are full of interesting melodies, harmonies, and rhythms. Approach each song one section at a time and then assemble the sections together in a sequence. This technique helps to provide you with a greater understanding of how the song is structured, and enables you to play it through more quickly.

In order to follow the music and my performance notes, you need a basic understanding of scales and chords. You may find the following chart helpful as you study the songs and performance notes. For each of the 12 major keys, it shows the basic chords built on that key's seven scale steps.

	1	2	3	4	5	6	7
A♭	A♭	B♭m	Cm	D♭	E♭	Fm	Gdim
A	A	Bm	C♯m	D	E	F♯m	G♯dim
B♭	B♭	Cm	Dm	E♭	F	Gm	Adim
B	B	C♯m	D♯m	E	F♯	G♯m	A♯dim
C	C	Dm	Em	F	G	Am	Bdim
D♭	D♭	E♭m	Fm	G♭	A♭	B♭m	Cdim
D	D	Em	F♯m	G	A	Bm	C♯dim
E♭	E♭	Fm	Gm	A♭	B♭	Cm	Ddim
E	E	F♯m	G♯m	A	B	C♯m	D♯dim
F	F	Gm	Am	B♭	C	Dm	Edim
F♯	F♯	G♯m	A♯m	B	C♯	D♯m	E♯dim
G	G	Am	Bm	C	D	Em	F♯dim

But if you're not a theory wiz, don't worry. Just spend a little time with the nifty tome *Music Theory For Dummies* by Michael Pilhofer and Holly Day (Wiley), and with a little practice, you're on your way to entertaining family and friends at your next social gathering.

Glossary

The songs and performance notes in this book use quite a number of musical terms that may be unfamiliar to you, so this section defines them for you in case you need to look something up in a jiffy:

- ✔ **Arpeggio:** Playing the notes of a chord one at a time rather than all together

- ✔ **Bridge:** Part of the song that is different from the verse and the chorus, providing variety and connecting the other parts of the song to each other

- ✔ **Coda:** The section at the end of a song, which is sometimes labeled with the word "coda"

- ✔ **Chorus:** The part of the song that is the same each time through, usually the most familiar section

- ✔ **Chromatic:** Moving by half steps, as in the example of C–B–B♭–A–A♭–G

- ✔ **Hook:** A familiar, accessible, or singalong melody, lick, or other section of the song

- ✔ **Progression:** A series of chords played in succession

- ✔ **Resolution:** A type of progression that creates a sense of closure

- ✔ **Slash chord:** A chord with a specific bass note listed to the right of the chord name — C/G, for example

- ✔ **Suspended chord:** Also known as a sus chord: a chord where the 3rd has been raised to the 4th

- ✔ **Verse:** The part of the song that tells the story; each verse has different lyrics, and each song generally has between two and four of these

Icons Used in This Book

In the margins of this book are lots of little icons that will help make your life easier:

A reason to stop and review advice that can prevent personal injury to your fingers, your brain, or your ego.

Optional parts, or alternate approaches, that those who'd like to find their way through the song with a distinctive flair can take. Often these strategies are slightly more challenging routes, but encouraged nonetheless, because there's nothing like a good challenge!

Notes about specific musical concepts that are relevant but confusing to non-musical types — stuff that you wouldn't bring up, say, at a frat party or at your kid's soccer game.

You get lots of these tips, because the more playing suggestions I can offer, the better you'll play. And isn't that what it's all about?

Shortcuts and techniques that you can take that help, well, *save time.*

All I Ask Of You

from THE PHANTOM OF THE OPERA
Music by Andrew Lloyd Webber
Lyrics by Charles Hart
Additional Lyrics by Richard Stilgoe

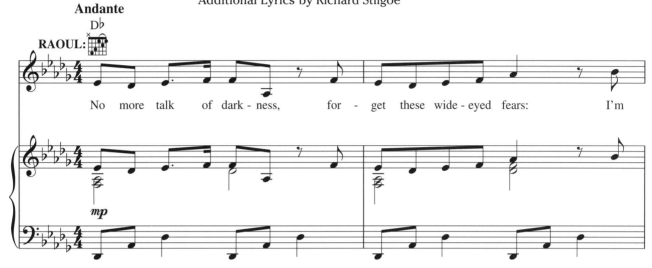

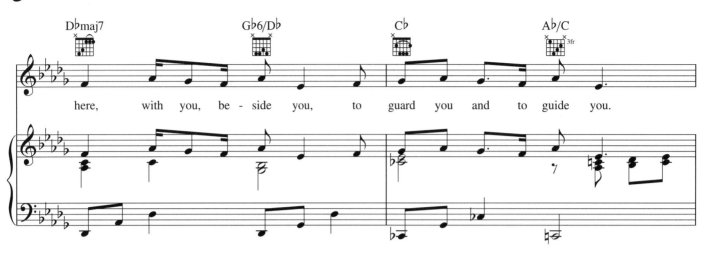

here,   with you,   be - side you,   to guard you and to guide you.

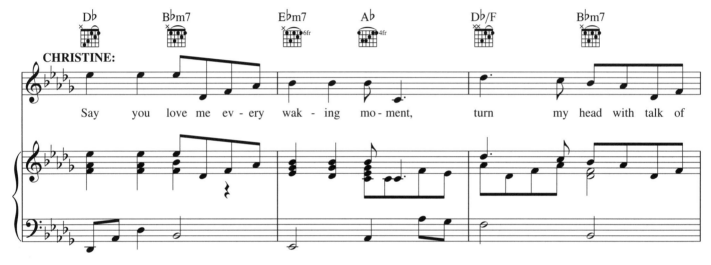

CHRISTINE:

Say   you love me ev - ery wak - ing mo - ment,   turn   my head with talk of

sum - mer - time.   Say   you need me with you now   and   al - ways;

prom - ise me   that all   you   say is   true,   that's all   I   ask of

rit.

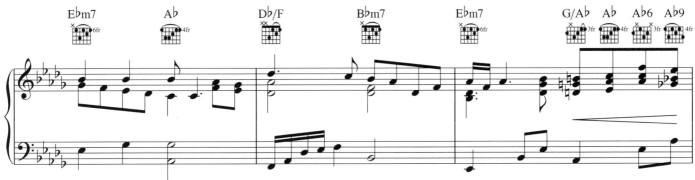

Always Look On The Bright Side Of Life

from MONTY PYTHON'S SPAMALOT
Words and Music by Eric Idle

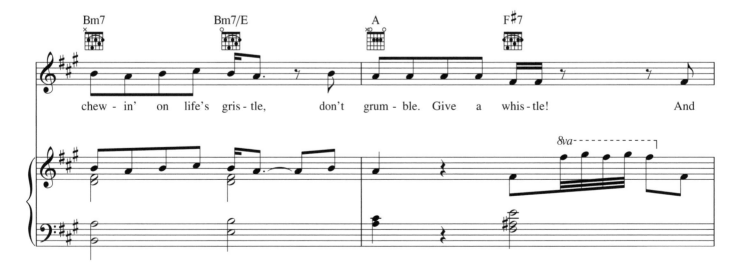

Some things in life are bad. They can real-ly make you mad.

Oth-er things just make you swear and curse. When you're

chew-in' on life's gris-tle, don't grum-ble. Give a whis-tle! And

Cheerful Soft-Shoe (♫ = ♩♪)

Add KNIGHTS (2nd time):

this-'ll help things turn out for the best... And, al - ways look on the

bright side __ of life. *(whistle)*

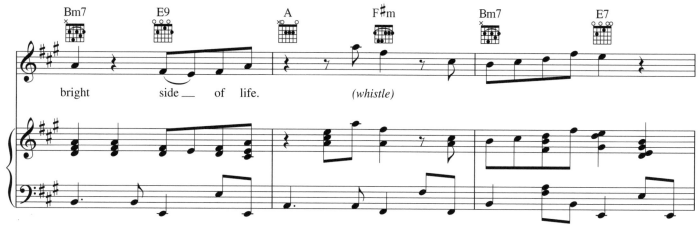

Al - ways look on the right side __ of life. *(whistle)*

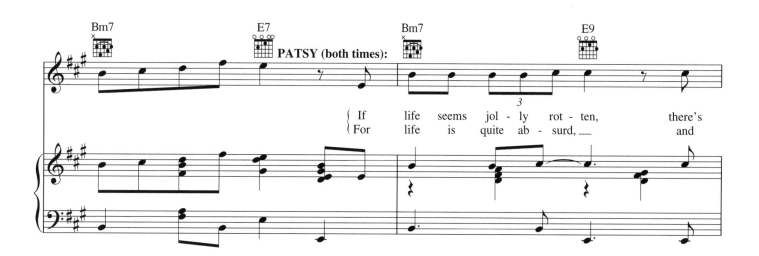

PATSY (both times):

{ If life seems jol - ly rot - ten, there's
{ For life is quite ab - surd, __ and

some - thing you've for - got - ten, and that's to laugh and smile and dance and
death's the fi - nal word. You must al - ways face the cur - tain with a

sing.
bow!
When you're feel - ing in the dumps, don't be sil - ly chumps. __ Just
For - get a - bout your sin. Give the au - di - ence a grin. ___ En -

purse your lips and whis - tle, that's the thing! And,
joy it, it's your last chance an - y - how!

ARTHUR:

Al - ways look on the bright side __ of death, *(whistle)*

Just be - fore you draw your ter - min - al breath.

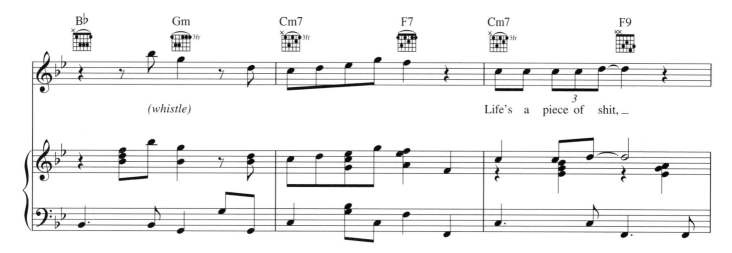

(whistle)   Life's a piece of shit, __

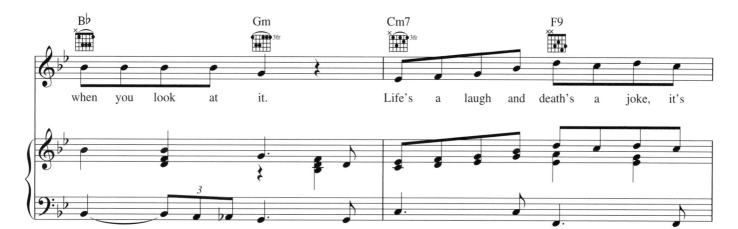

when you look at it.   Life's a laugh and death's a joke, it's

true.   **PATSY:** You'll see it's all a show. Keep 'em laugh - ing as you go! __ **ARTHUR:** Just re -

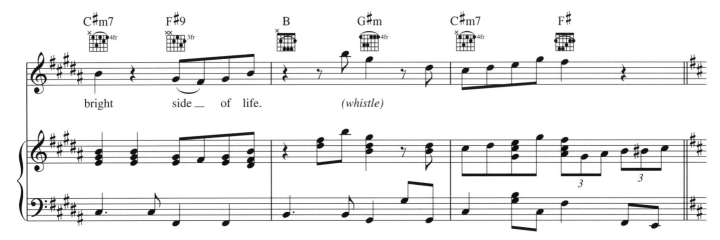

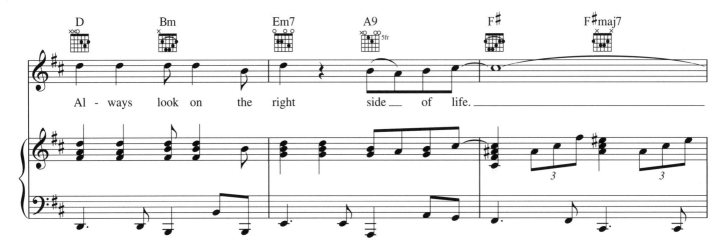

death's the fi - nal word. You must al - ways face the cur - tain with a

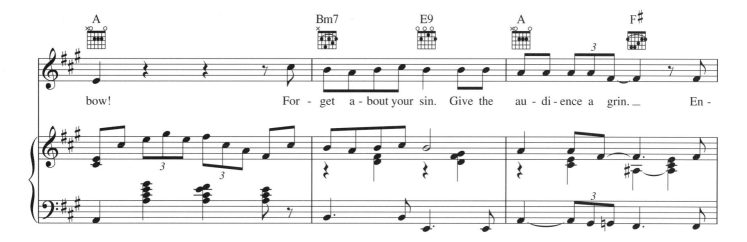

bow! For - get a - bout your sin. Give the au - di - ence a grin. ___ En -

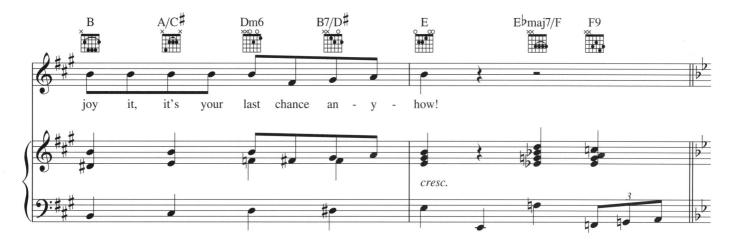

joy it, it's your last chance an - y - how!

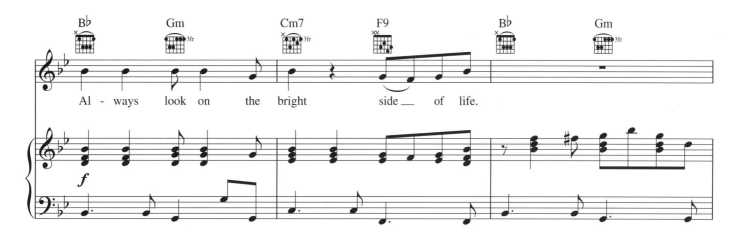

Al - ways look on the bright side ___ of life.

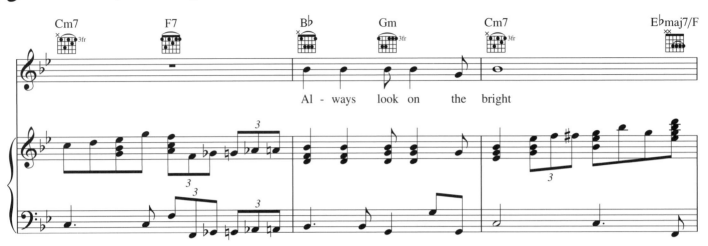

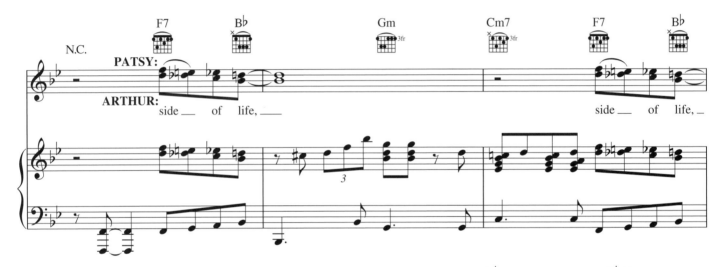

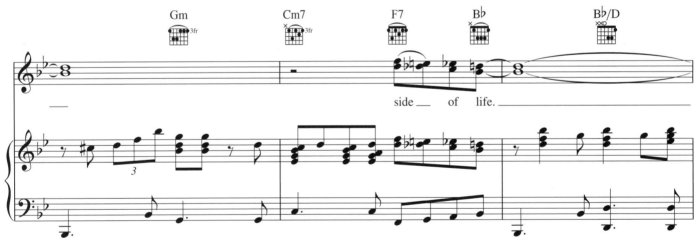

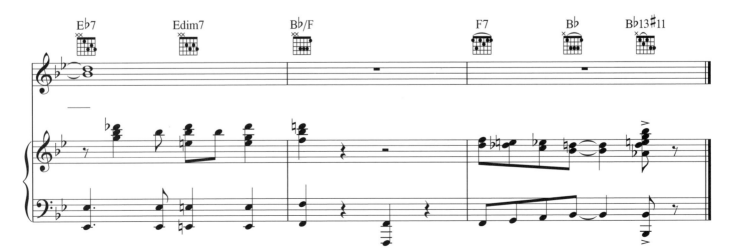

Another Op'nin', Another Show

from KISS ME, KATE
Words and Music by Cole Porter

Allegro (very lively)

An - oth - er op' - nin', an -

oth - er show, ____ In Phil - ly, Bos - ton or

Bal - ti - mo'e, ____ A chance for stage - folks to

say "hel - lo" ___ An - oth - er op' - nin' of

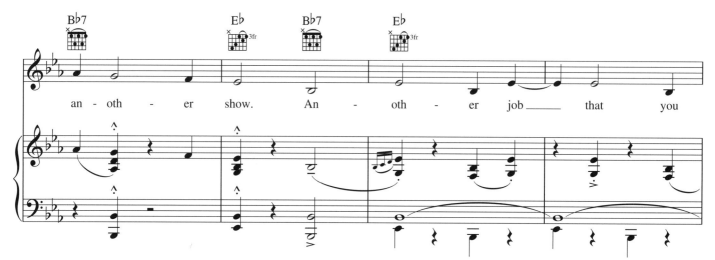

an - oth - er show. An - oth - er job ___ that you

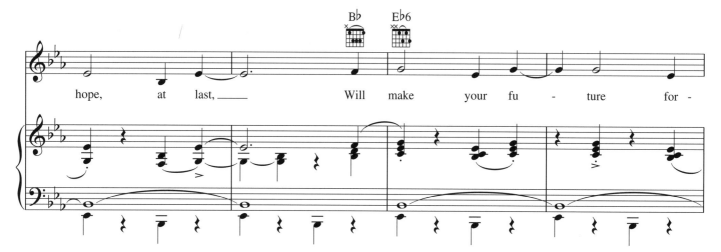

hope, at last, ___ Will make your fu - ture for -

get your past, ___ An - oth - er pain ___ where the

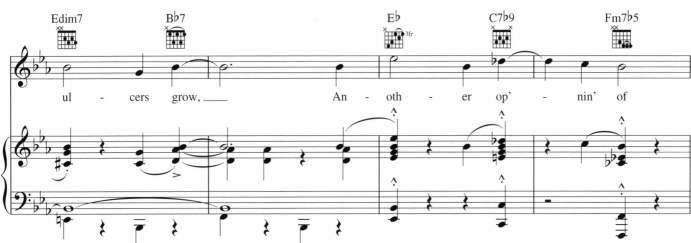

ul - cers grow, ___ An - oth - er op' - nin' of

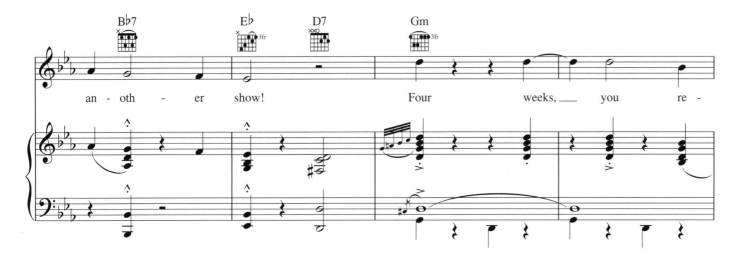

an - oth - er show! Four weeks, ___ you re -

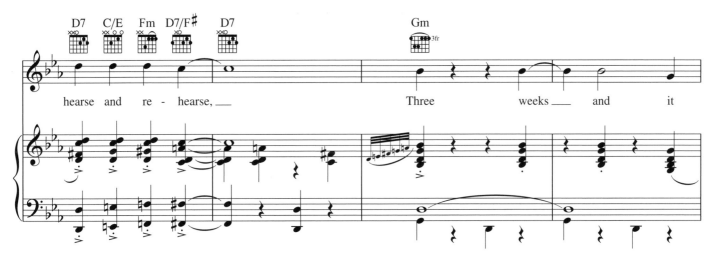

hearse and re - hearse, ___ Three weeks ___ and it

could - n't be worse. ___ One week, ___ will it

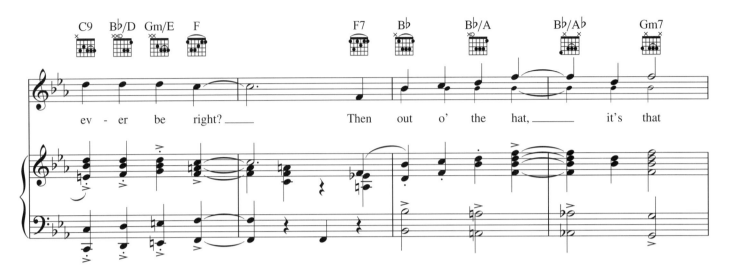

ev - er be right? _____ Then out o' the hat, _____ it's that

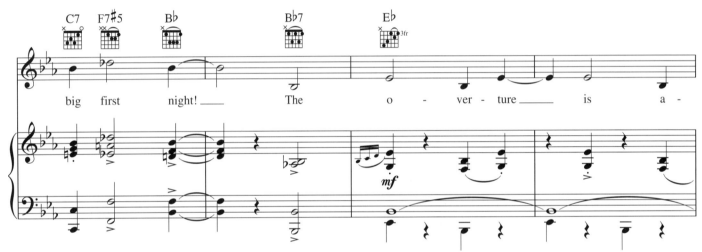

big first night! _____ The o - ver - ture _____ is a -

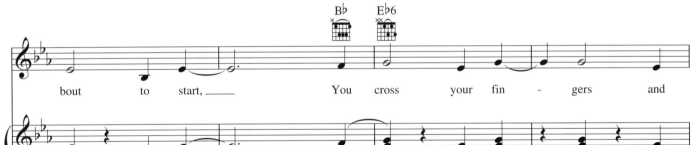

bout to start, _____ You cross your fin - gers and

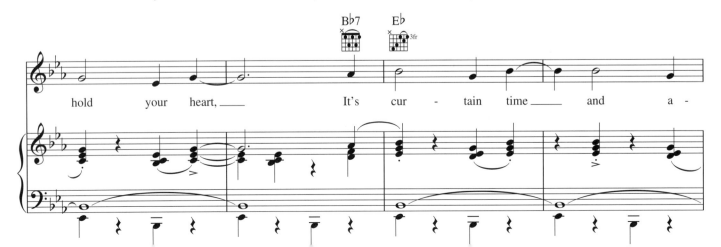

hold your heart, _____ It's cur - tain time _____ and a -

Any Dream Will Do

from JOSEPH AND THE AMAZING TECHNICOLOR DREAMCOAT
Music by Andrew Lloyd Webber
Lyrics by Tim Rice

way some - one was weep - ing,

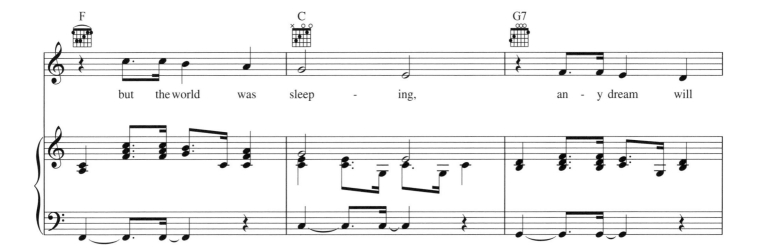

but the world was sleep - ing, an - y dream will

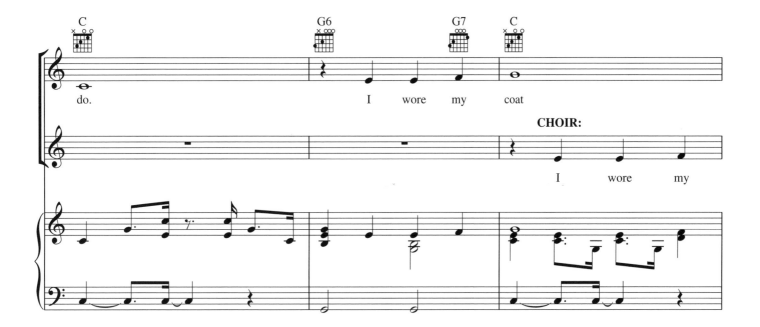

do. I wore my coat

CHOIR:

I wore my

with gold - en lin - ing, bright col - ours
coat, ah,

shin - ing won - der - ful and new.
ah,

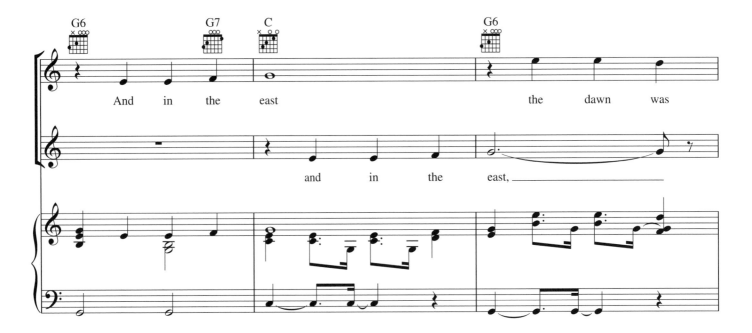

And in the east the dawn was
and in the east,

break - ing, and the world was wak - ing, ah, _____ ah, ___

an - y dream will do. _____

JOSEPH:

A

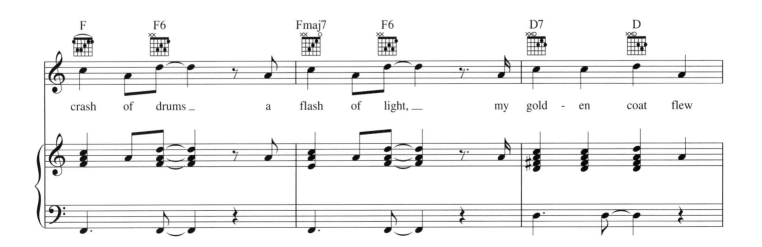

crash of drums _ a flash of light, _ my gold - en coat flew

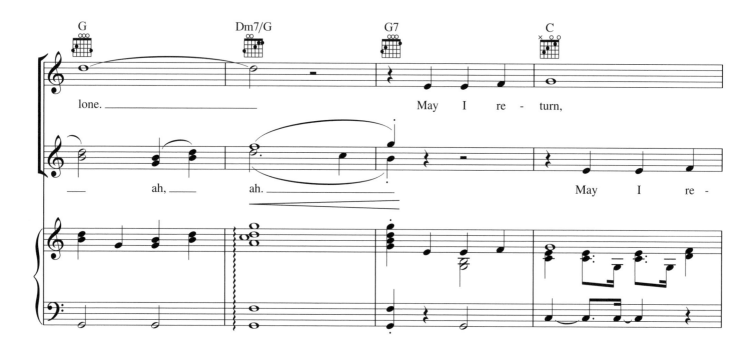

dim - ming   and the dream is   too,

ah. _____

the world and   I,   we are still

The   world   and   I, _____

wait - ing,   still hes - i - tat - ing

ah, _____   ah. ____

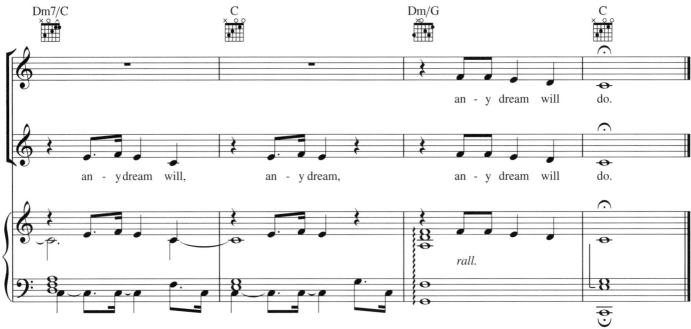

Big Spender

from SWEET CHARITY
Words by Dorothy Fields   Music by Cy Coleman

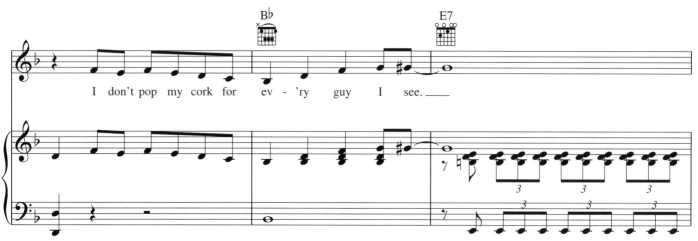

I don't pop my cork for ev - 'ry guy I see. ____

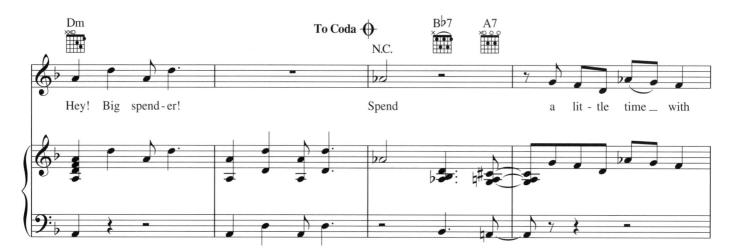

Hey! Big spend - er!   Spend   a lit - tle time __ with

me.   Do you like to have

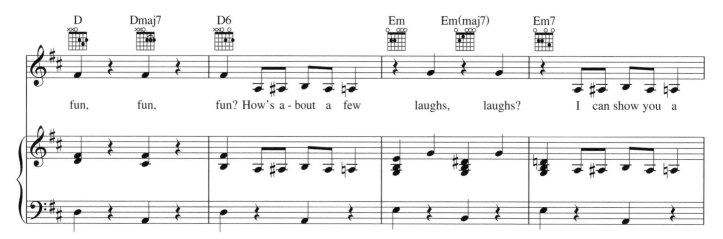

fun,   fun,   fun? How's a - bout a few   laughs,   laughs?   I can show you a

good time. _____ Let me show you a good time. _____ The min-ute you

Hey, big spend-er! Hey, big spend-er!

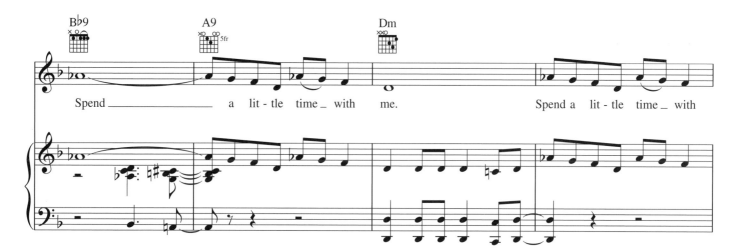

Spend _____ a lit-tle time _ with me. Spend a lit-tle time _ with

me. Spend a lit-tle time _ with me. _____

As Long As He Needs Me

from the Broadway Musical OLIVER!
Words and Music by Lionel Bart

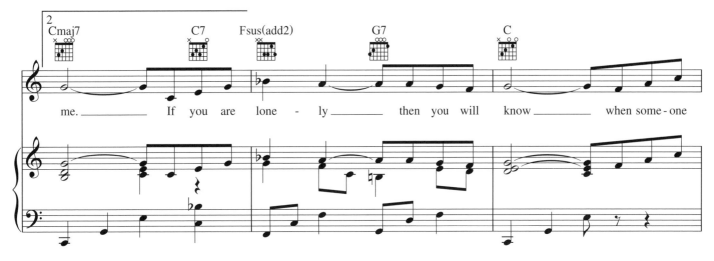

me. _____ If you are lone - ly _____ then you will know _____ when some - one

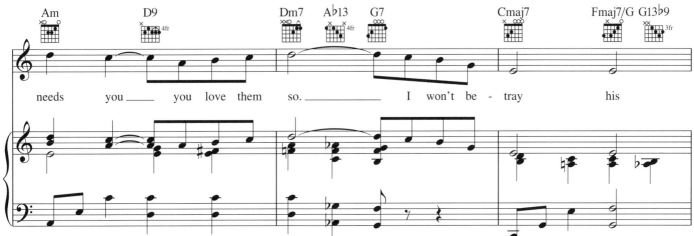

needs you _____ you love them so. _____ I won't be - tray his

trust, _____ though peo - ple say I must. _____ I've got to

stay true, just _____ as long as he needs me.

Cabaret

from the Musical CABARET
Words by Fred Ebb   Music by John Kander

cab - a - ret, old chum, _____

come to the cab - a - ret. _____

ret. Come taste the wine, come hear the

band, come blow the horn, start cel - e - brat - ing,

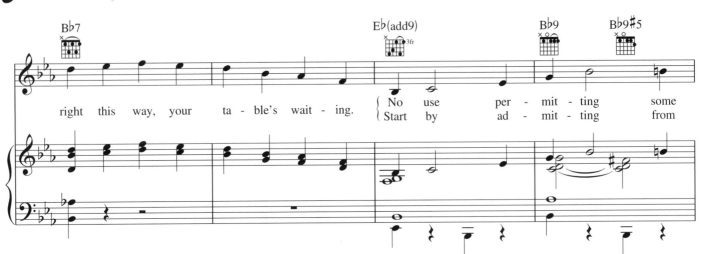

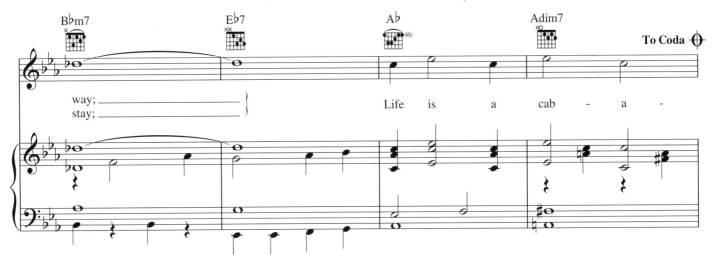

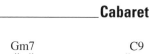

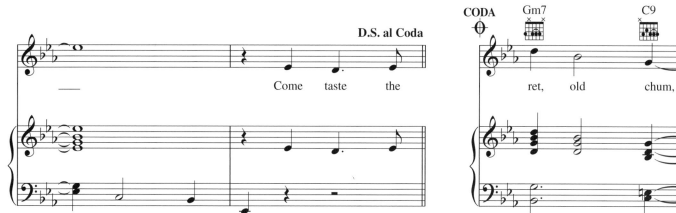

Come taste the

ret, old chum, ___

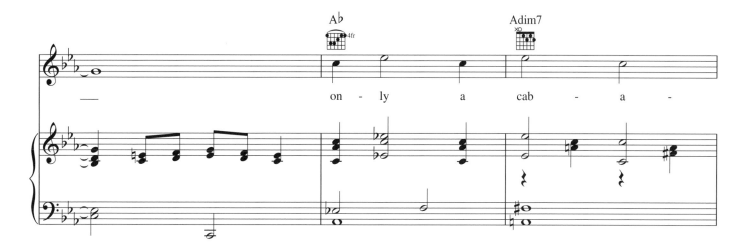

___ on - ly a cab - a -

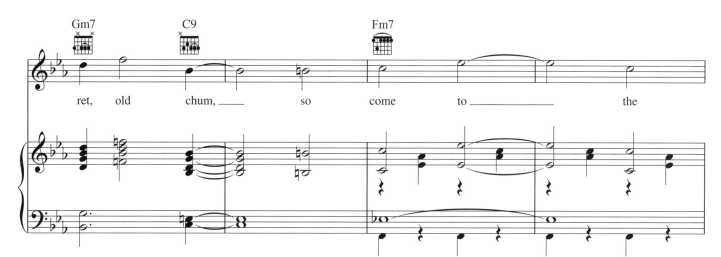

ret, old chum, ____ so come to _____ the

cab - a - ret. _____

Camelot

Words and Music by Credits

D#dim7　　C7

lim - it to the snow here _____ in

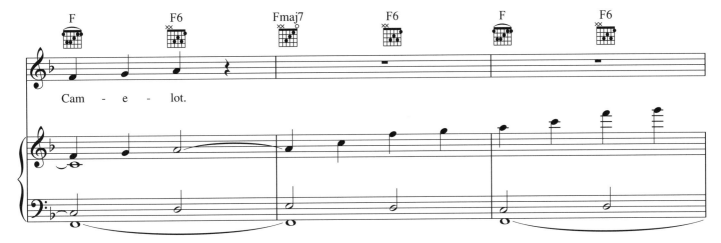

F　F6　Fmaj7　F6　F　F6

Cam - e - lot.

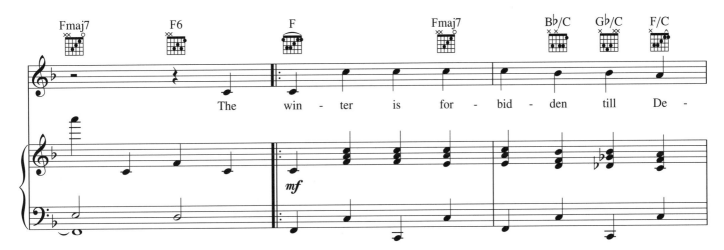

Fmaj7　F6　F　Fmaj7　Bb/C　Gb/C　F/C

The win - ter is for - bid - den till De -

mf

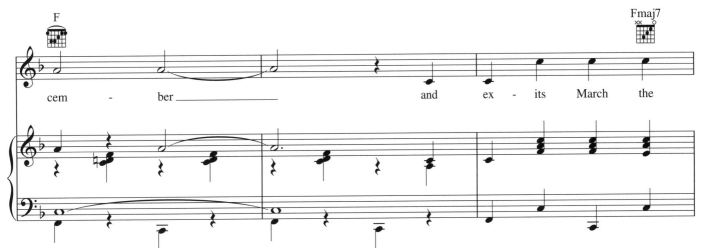

F　　　　　　　　　　　　　　　　　Fmaj7

cem - ber _____ and ex - its March the

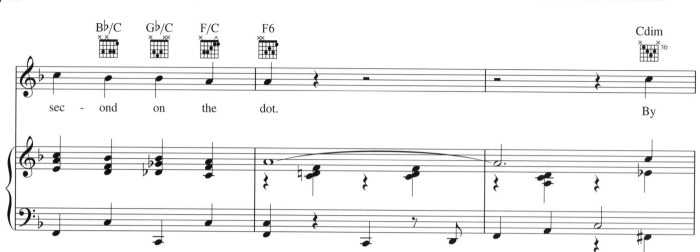

sec - ond on the dot.

By

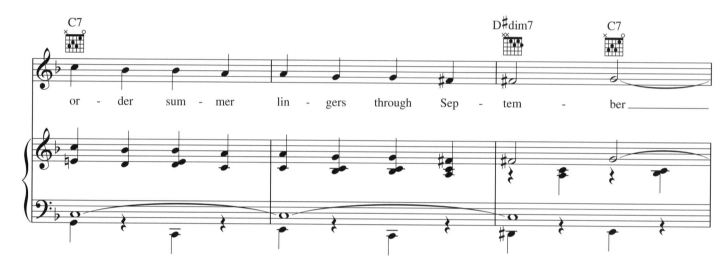

or - der sum - mer lin - gers through Sep - tem - ber

in Cam - e - lot.

Cam - e - lot!

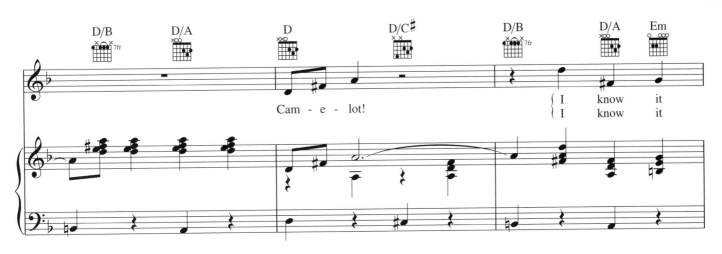

Cam - e - lot!

I know it
I know it

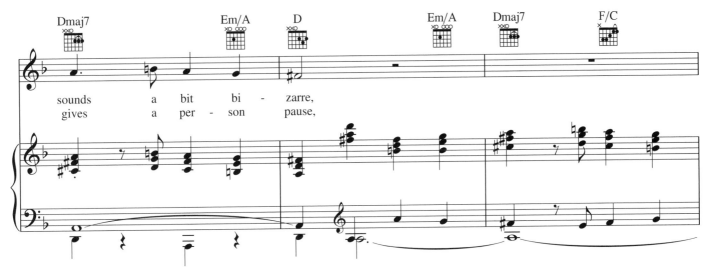

sounds a bit bi - zarre,
gives a per - son pause,

but in Cam - e - lot,
but in Cam - e - lot,

Cam - e - lot,
Cam - e - lot,

that's how con - di - tions
those are the le - gal

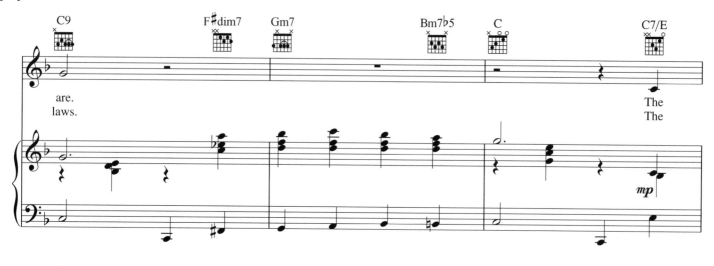

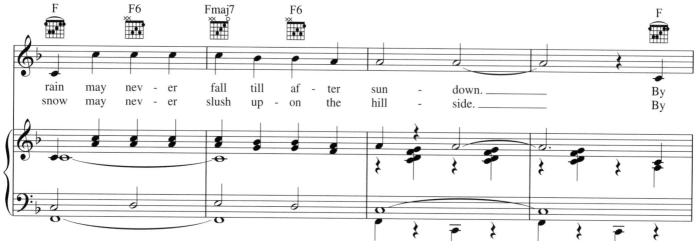

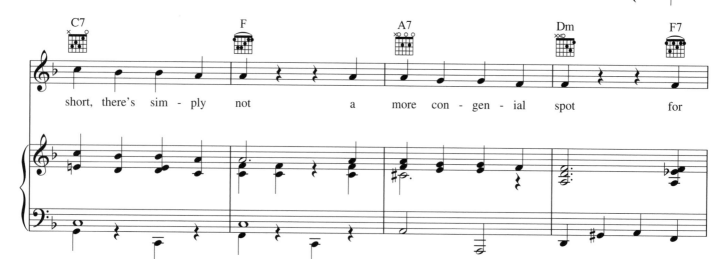

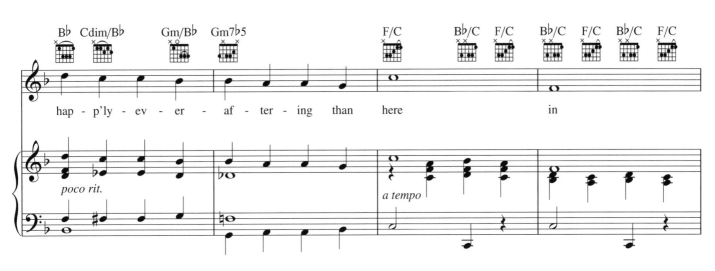

hap - p'ly - ev - er - af - ter - ing than here in

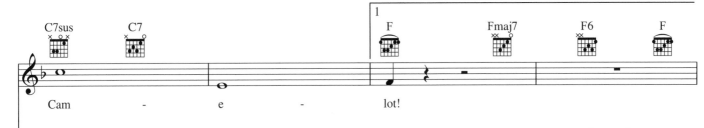

Cam - e - lot!

The lot!

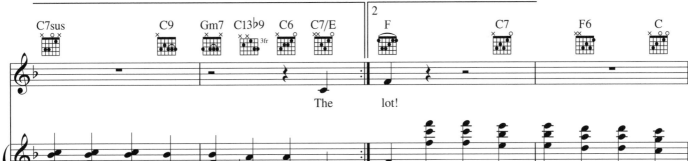

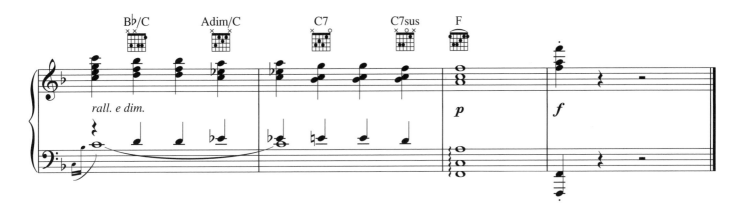

Can You Feel The Love Tonight

Disney Presents THE LION KING: THE BROADWAY MUSICAL
Music by Elton John
Lyrics by Tim Rice

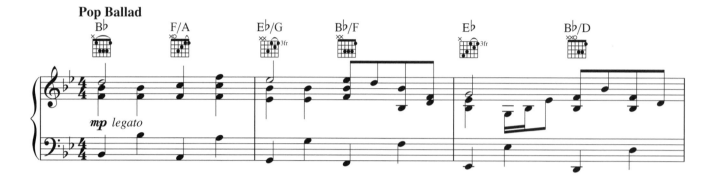

There's a calm __ sur-ren __ - der
There's a time __ for ev - 'ry - one,

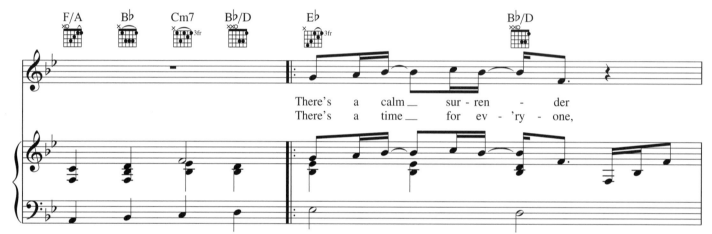

to the rush __ of day, __ when the heat __ of the roll-ing world __
if they on - ly learn __ that the twist - ing ka - lei-do - scope __

can be turned __ a - way. __ An en - chant - ed mo - ment,
moves us all __ in turn. __ There's a rhyme __ and rea - son

and it sees ___ me through. It's e - nough ___ for this rest - less war - rior
to the wild ___ out - doors ___ when the heart ___ of this star - crossed voy - ag - er

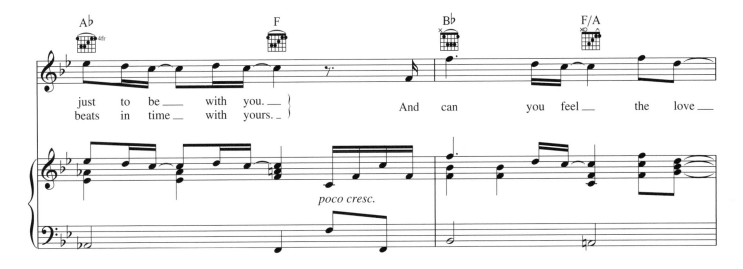

just to be ___ with you. ___ And can you feel ___ the love ___
beats in time ___ with yours. ___

poco cresc.

___ to - night? ___ It is where ___ we are. ___

It's e - nough _____ for this

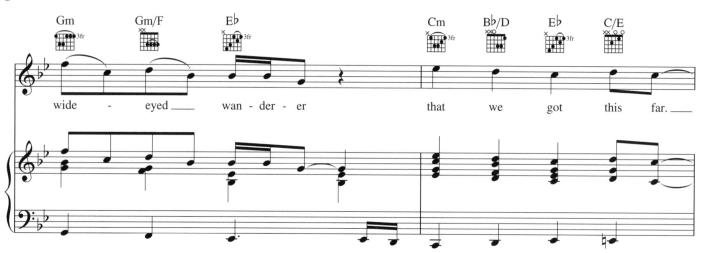

wide - eyed ____ wan - der - er that we got this far. ____

____ And can you feel ____ the love ____

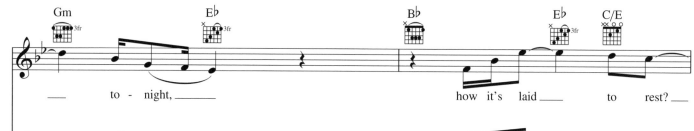

____ to - night, _____ how it's laid ____ to rest? ____

____ It's e - nough _____ to make

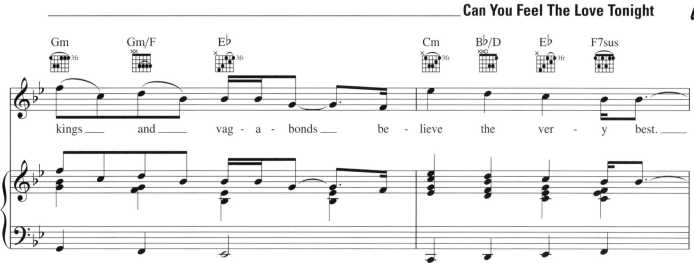

kings ___ and ___ vag - a - bonds ___ be - lieve the ver - y best. ___

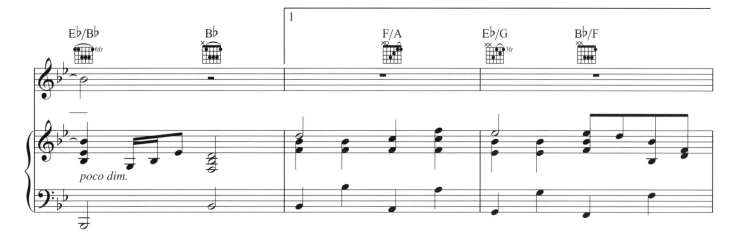

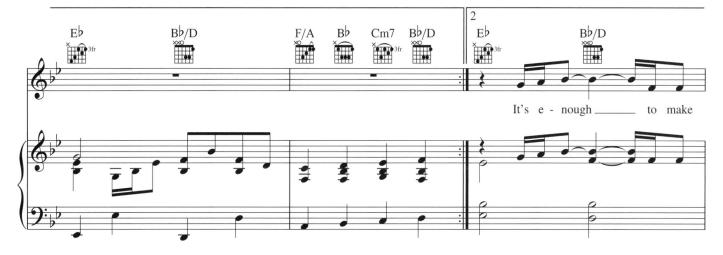

It's e - nough ___ to make

kings ___ and ___ vag - a - bonds ___ be - lieve the ver - y best. ___

Don't Cry For Me Argentina

from EVITA
Words by Tim Rice
Music by Andrew Lloyd Webber

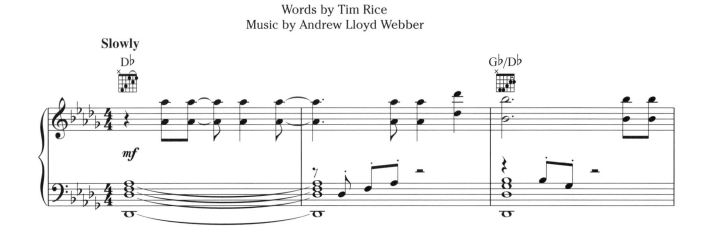

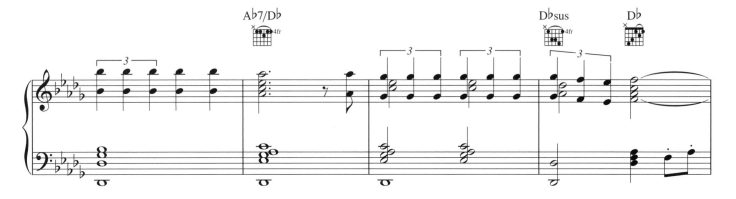

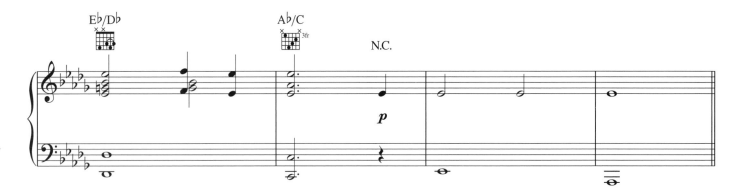

EVA:
It won't be eas - y, you'll think it strange when I

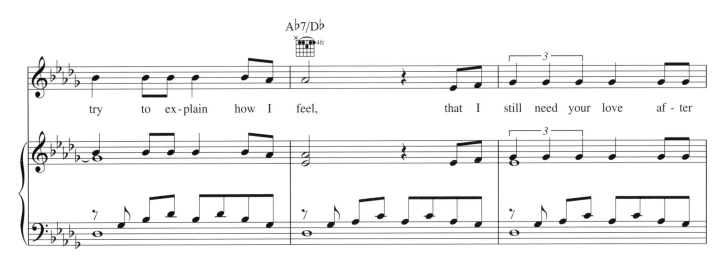

try to ex - plain how I feel, that I still need your love af - ter

all that I've done. You won't be - lieve me.

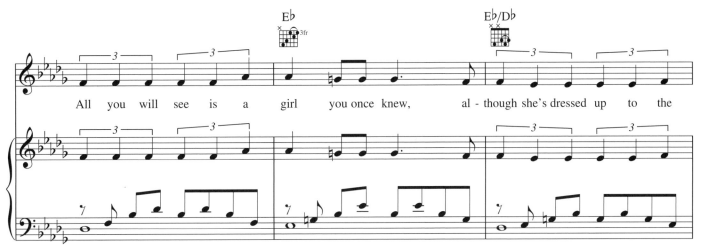

All you will see is a girl you once knew, al - though she's dressed up to the

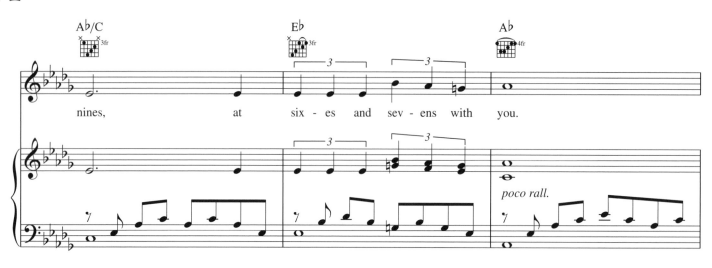

nines,   at   six - es   and   sev - ens   with   you.

I had to let it hap - pen, I had to change,   could - n't spend all my life down at

heel,   look - ing out of the win - dow, stay - ing out of the sun.   So I chose

free - dom,   run - ning a - round try - ing ev - 'ry - thing new,   but noth - ing im - pressed me at all, ___

I nev - er ex - pec - ted it to.

rall.

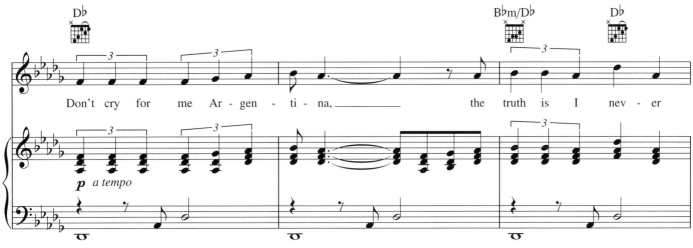

Don't cry for me Ar - gen - ti - na, _____ the truth is I nev - er

p a tempo

left you. All through my wild days, _____ my mad ex - is - tence, _____ I kept my

prom - ise, don't keep your dis - tance. _____

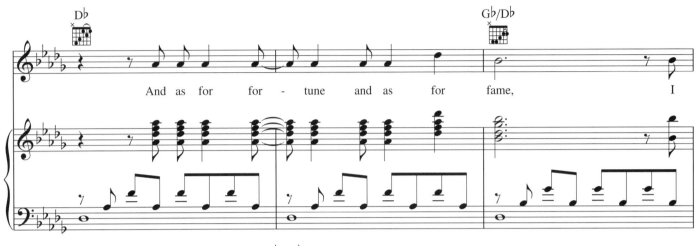

And as for for - tune and as for fame,

I

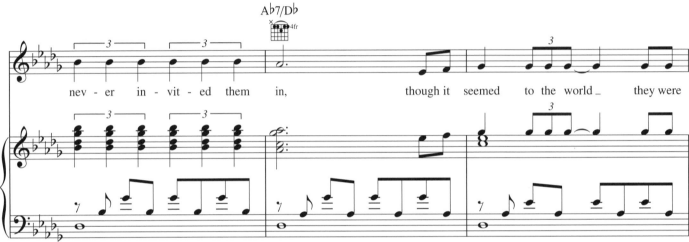

nev - er in - vit - ed them in, though it seemed to the world _ they were

all I de - sired. They are il - lu - sions, they're

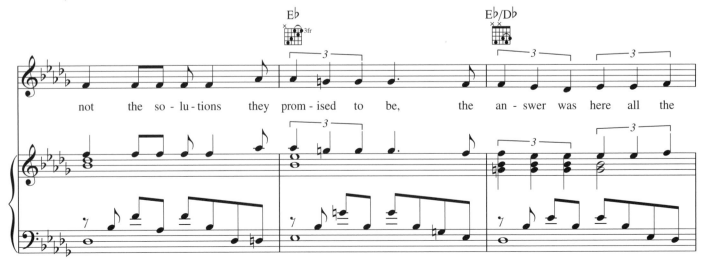

not the so - lu - tions they prom - ised to be, the an - swer was here all the

time, I love you and hope you love me.

Don't cry for me Ar - gen - ti - na. **CHOIR:** Mm

a tempo

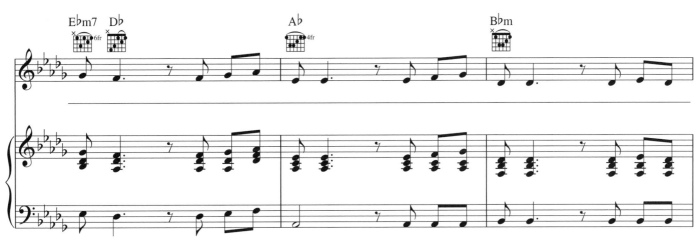

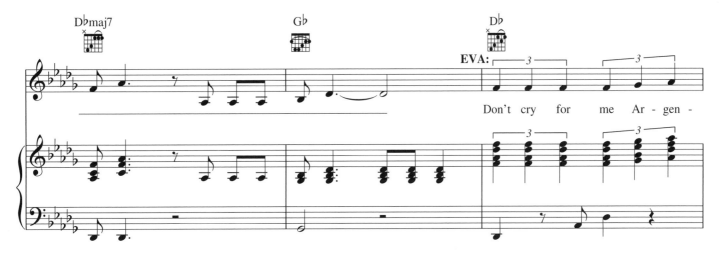

EVA: Don't cry for me Ar - gen -

ti - na, _____ the truth is I nev - er left you. All through my

wild days, _____ my mad ex - is - tence, I kept my prom - ise, don't keep your

dis - tance. _____ Have I said too much, there's noth - ing more I can think of to

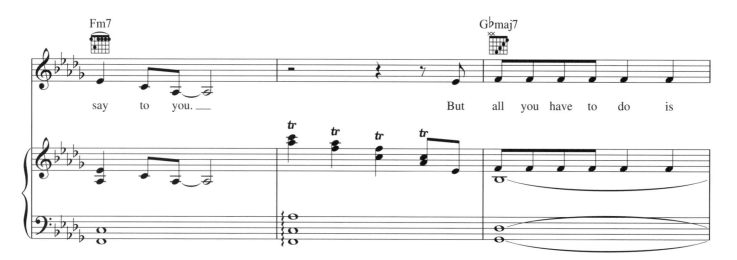

say to you. ___ But all you have to do is

look at me to know that ev-'ry word is true. __

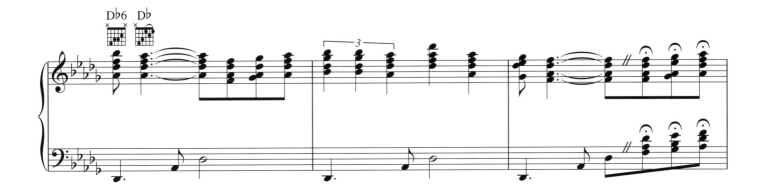

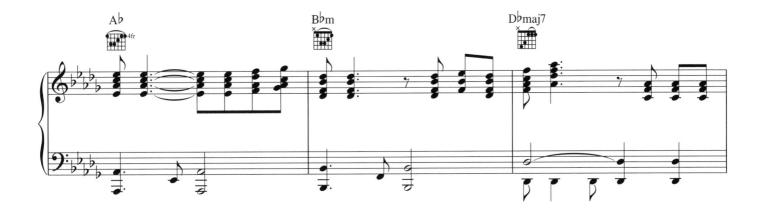

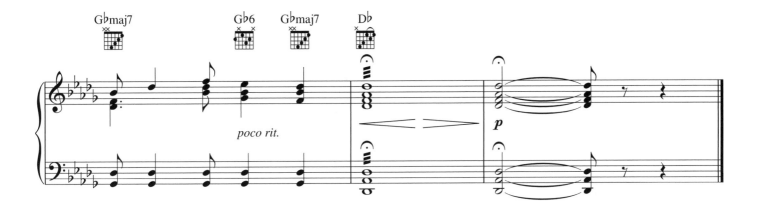

poco rit.

Everything's Alright

from JESUS CHRIST SUPERSTAR
Words by Tim Rice
Music by Andrew Lloyd Webber

Moderately

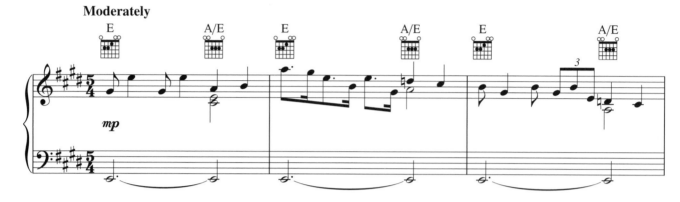

(1., D.S.) *Mary Magdalene:* Try not to get wor-ried, try not to turn on to
(2.) *Mary Magdalene:* Sleep and I shall soothe you, calm you and a-noint you,

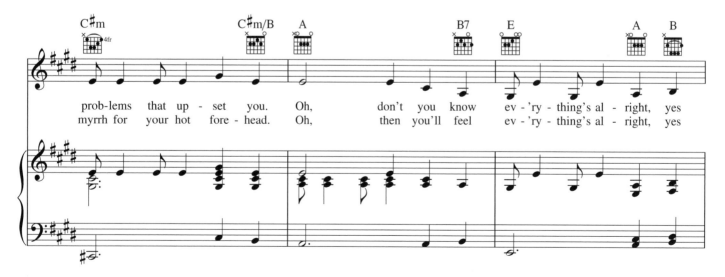

prob-lems that up-set you. Oh, don't you know ev-'ry-thing's al-right, yes
myrrh for your hot fore-head. Oh, then you'll feel ev-'ry-thing's al-right, yes

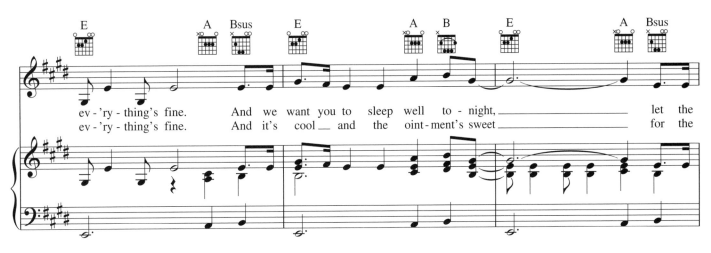

ev - 'ry - thing's fine. And we want you to sleep well to - night,_____ let the
ev - 'ry - thing's fine. And it's cool__ and the oint - ment's sweet_____ for the

world__ turn with - out you to - night._____ If we try we'll get by, so for-
fire__ in__ your head and feet._____ Close your eyes, close your eyes and re-

To Coda ⊕

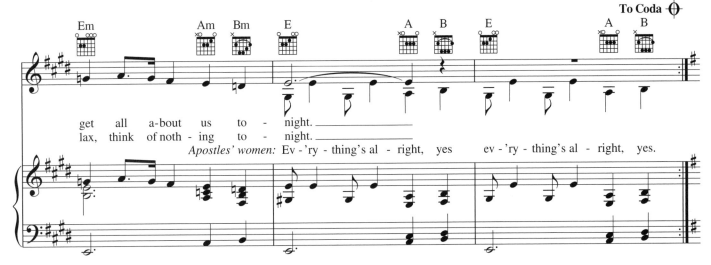

get all a - bout us to - night._____
lax, think of noth - ing to - night._____

Apostles' women: Ev - 'ry - thing's al - right, yes ev - 'ry - thing's al - right, yes.

Rock

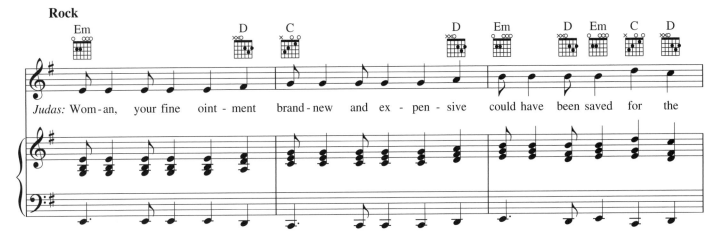

Judas: Wom - an, your fine oint - ment brand - new and ex - pen - sive could have been saved for the

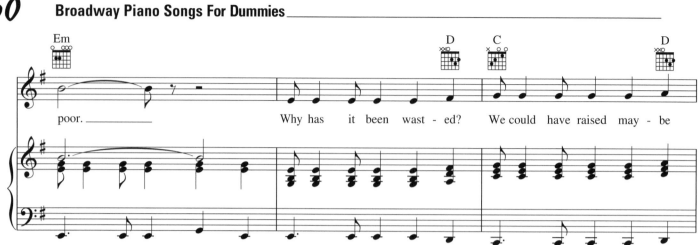

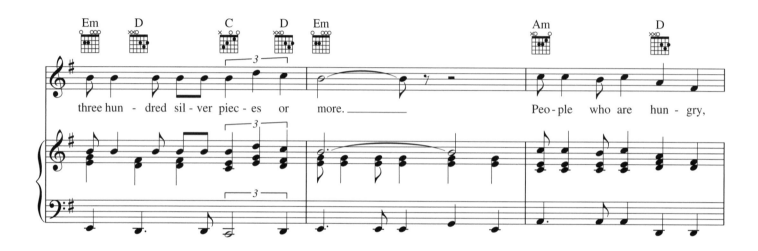

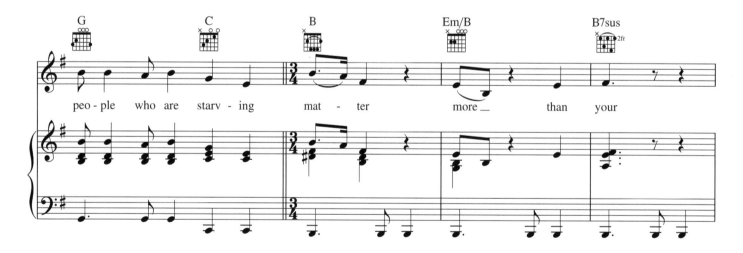

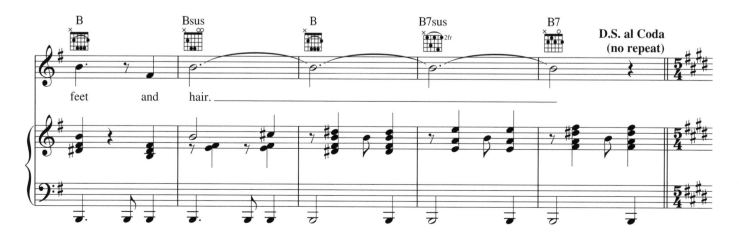

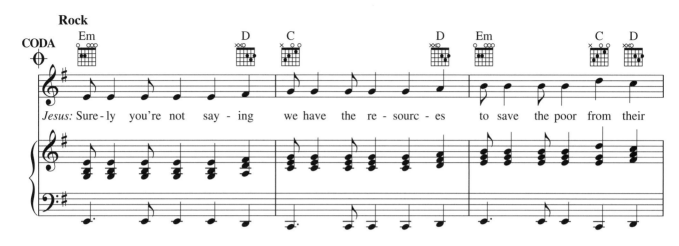

Rock

CODA

Em   D   C   D   Em   C D

Jesus: Sure - ly you're not say - ing we have the re - sourc - es to save the poor from their

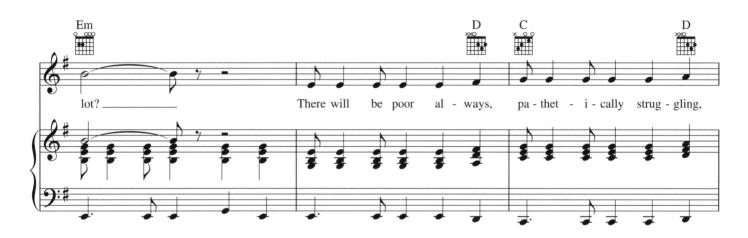

Em   D   C   D

lot? _____ There will be poor al - ways, pa - thet - i - cally strug - gling,

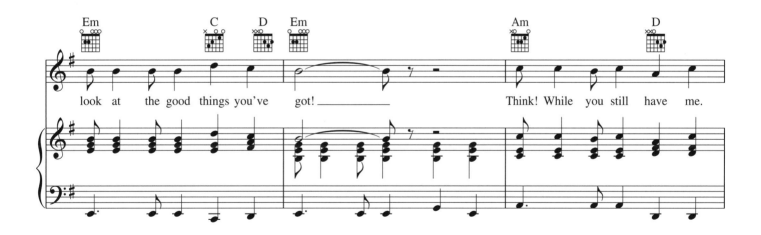

Em   C D Em   Am   D

look at the good things you've got! _____ Think! While you still have me.

G   C   B   Em/B

Move! While you still see me. You'll be lost, _____ you'll be

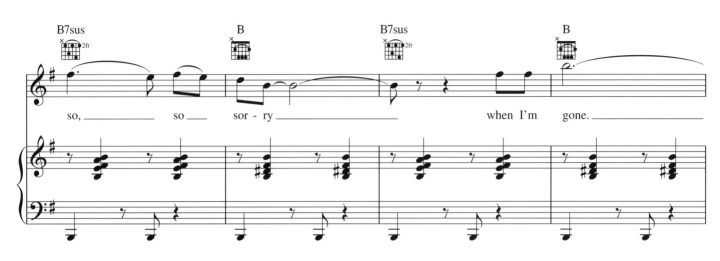

so, _____ so sor - ry _____ when I'm gone. _____

Light Rock

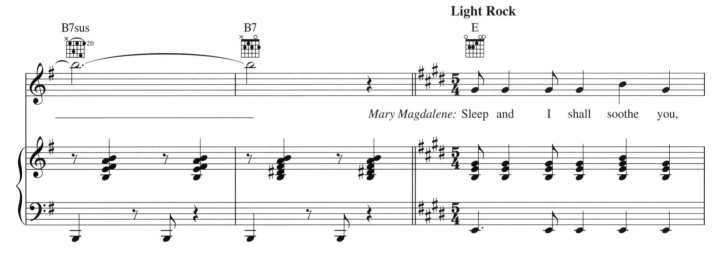

Mary Magdalene: Sleep and I shall soothe you,

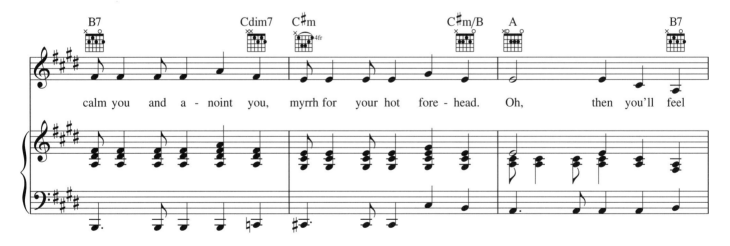

calm you and a - noint you, myrrh for your hot fore - head. Oh, then you'll feel

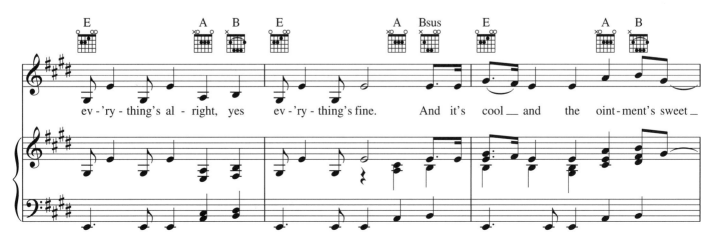

ev - 'ry - thing's al - right, yes ev - 'ry - thing's fine. And it's cool __ and the oint - ment's sweet __

for the fire ___ in your head and feet. ___   Close your

eyes,   close your eyes and re - lax, think of noth - ing   to - night. _____

Apostles' women: Close your eyes,   close your eyes and re-

Hard Rock   *Repeat many times, crescendo to **f**, then fade*

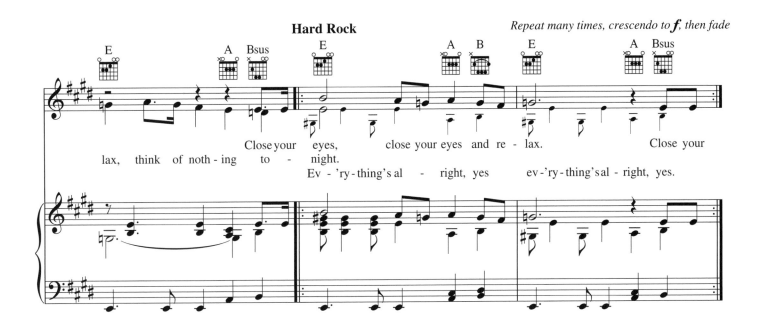

lax, think of noth - ing   to - night.   Close your eyes,   close your eyes and re - lax.   Close your

Ev - 'ry - thing's al - right, yes   ev - 'ry - thing's al - right, yes.

Everything's Coming Up Roses

from GYPSY
Words by Stephen Sondheim
Music by Jule Styne

Briskly

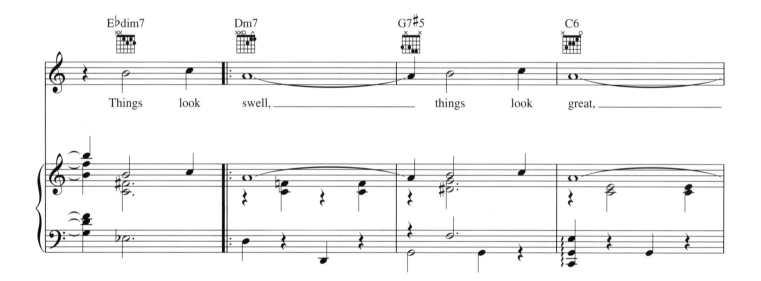

Things look swell, _____ things look great, _____

_____ gon - na have the whole world _____ on a plate. _____

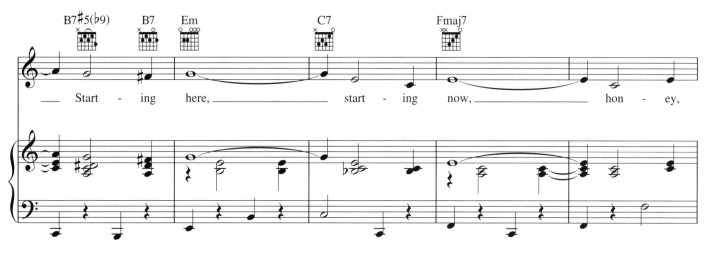

Start - ing here, _____ start - ing now, _____ hon - ey,

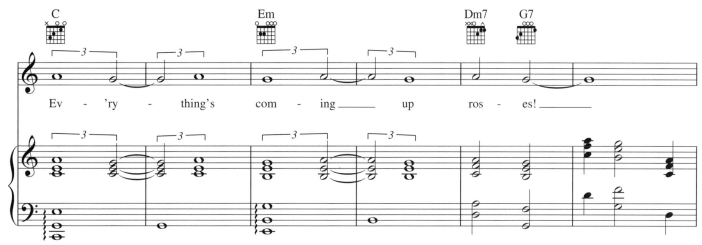

Ev - 'ry - thing's com - ing _____ up ros - es! _____

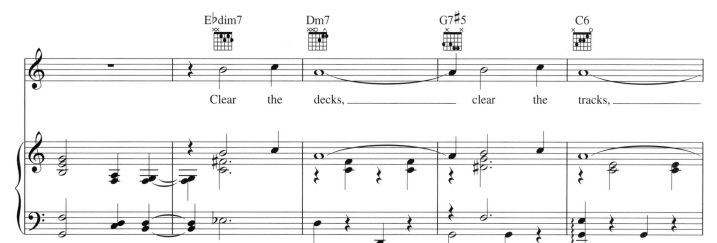

Clear the decks, _____ clear the tracks, _____

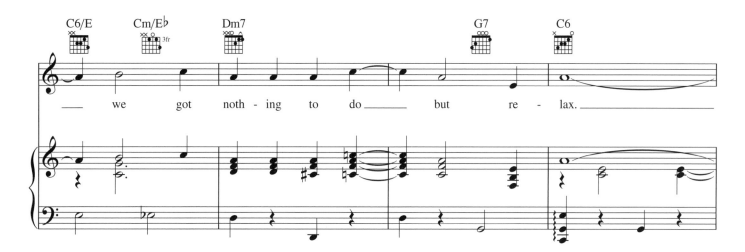

_____ we got noth - ing to do _____ but re - lax. _____

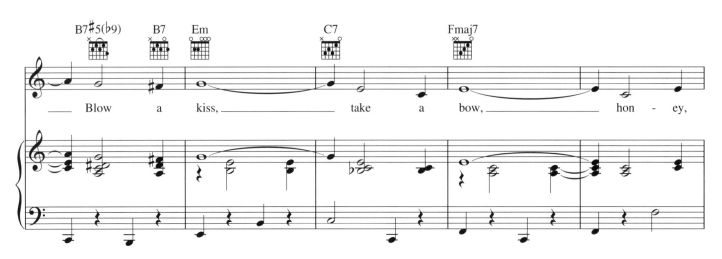

Blow a kiss, _____ take a bow, _____ hon - ey,

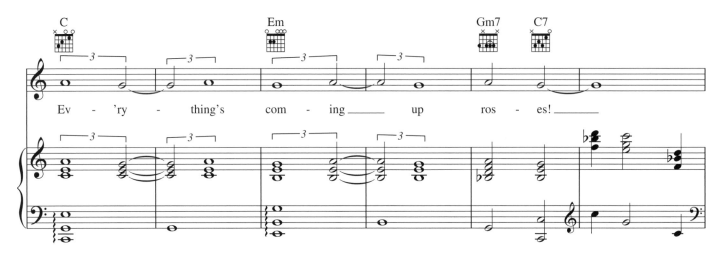

Ev - 'ry - thing's com - ing _____ up ros - es! _____

Now's our _____

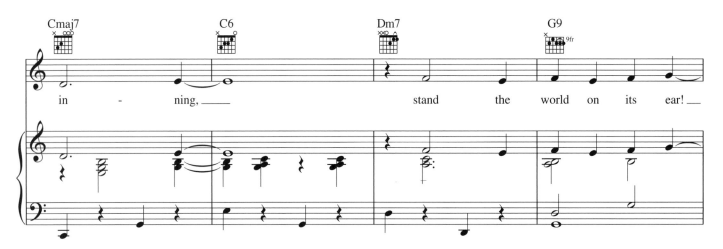

in - ning, _____ stand the world on its ear! _____

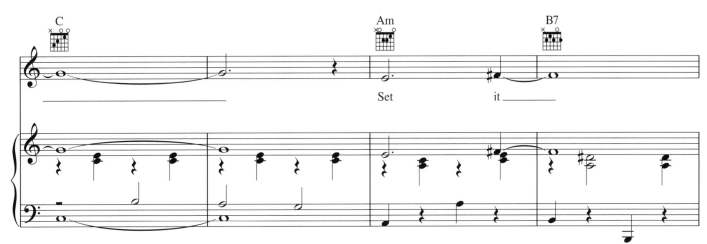

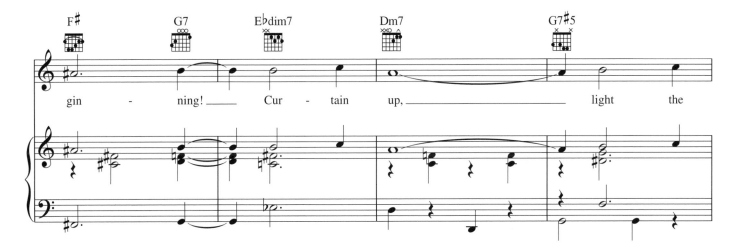

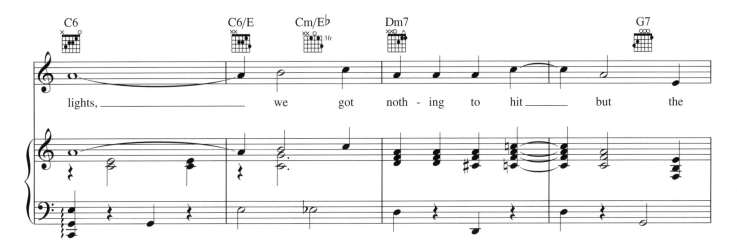

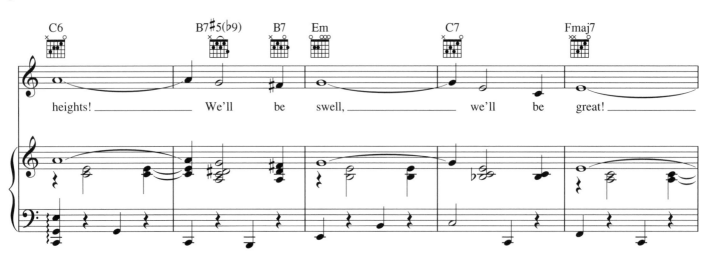

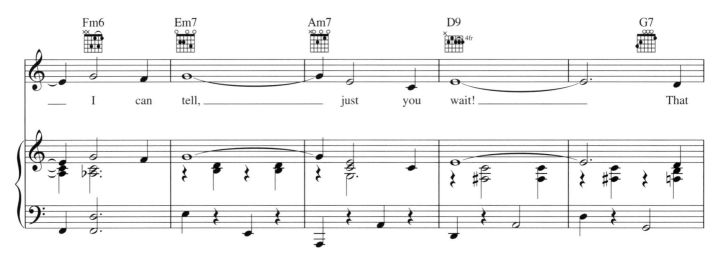

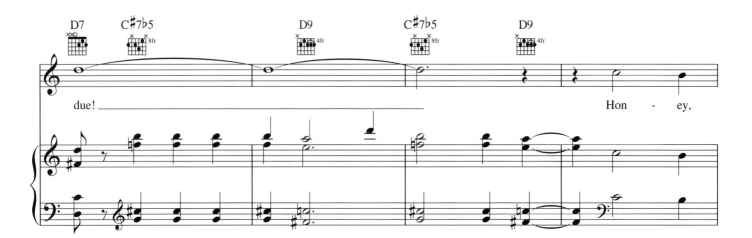

Gonna Build A Mountain

from the Musical Production STOP THE WORLD - I WANT TO GET OFF
Words and Music by Leslie Bricusse and Anthony Newley

Gon - na build a moun - tain
day - dream
heav - en from a lit - tle
from a lit - tle
from a lit - tle

hill.
hope.
hell.

Gon - na build a moun - tain,
Gon - na push that day - dream
Gon - na build a heav - en,

least I hope I will.
up the moun - tain slope.
and I know darn well,

Gon - na build a
Gon - na build a
if I build my

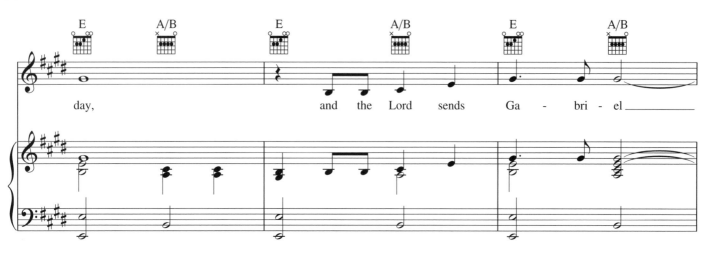

day, and the Lord sends Ga - bri - el

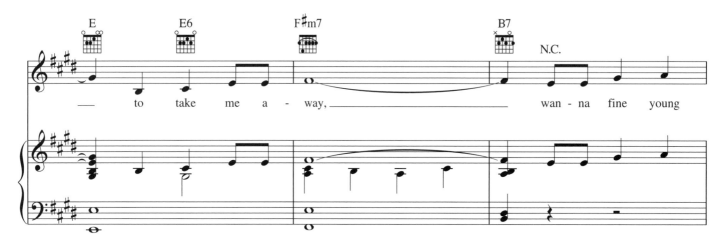

to take me a - way, wan - na fine young

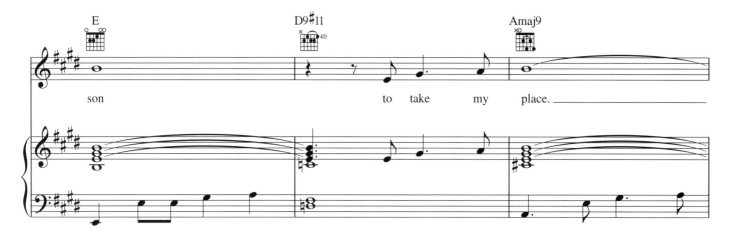

son to take my place.

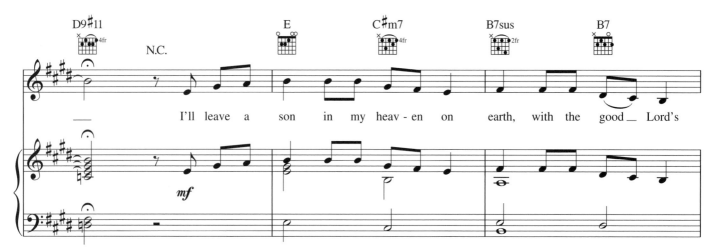

I'll leave a son in my heav - en on earth, with the good Lord's

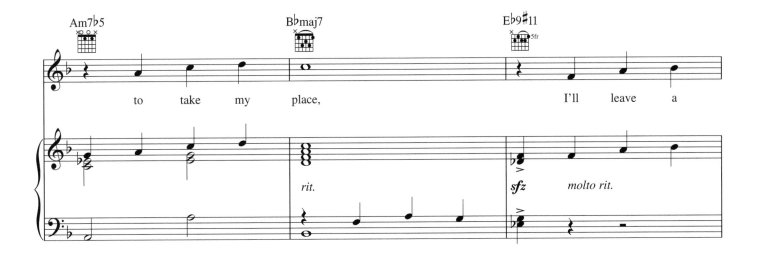

Extra Verses

Gonna build a heaven from a little hell.
Gonna build a heaven, and I know darn well,
With a fine young son to take my place
There'll be a sun in my heaven on earth
With the good Lord's grace.

Gonna build a mountain from a little hill.
Gonna build a mountain – least I hope I will.
Gonna build a mountain – gonna build it high.
I don't know how I'm gonna do it –
Only know I'm gonna try.

Hello, Dolly!

from HELLO, DOLLY!
Music and Lyric by Jerry Herman

lap,   fel - las. }
knee,   fel - las. }
Dol - ly - 'll nev - er   go   a - way a -

gain!   Hel - go   a - way,

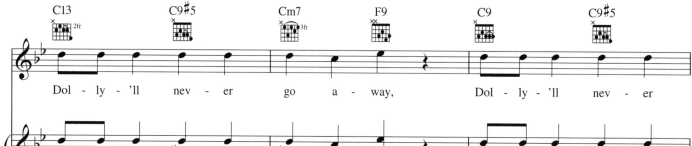

Dol - ly - 'll nev - er   go   a - way,   Dol - ly - 'll nev - er

go   a - way a - gain! _____

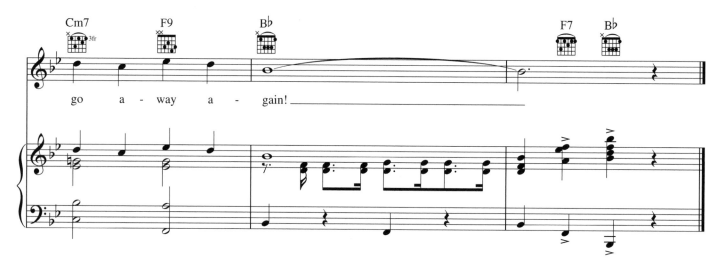

Hey, Look Me Over

from WILDCAT
Music by Cy Coleman
Lyrics by Carolyn Leigh

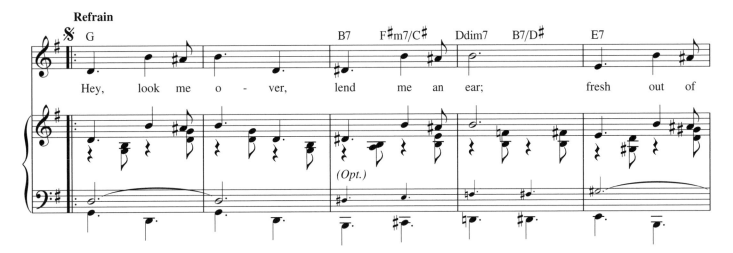

Hey, look me o- ver, lend me an ear; fresh out of

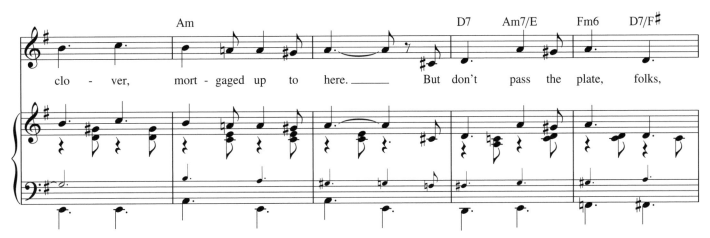

clo- ver, mort- gaged up to here. But don't pass the plate, folks,

don't pass the cup; I fig- ure when- ev- er you're down and out, the

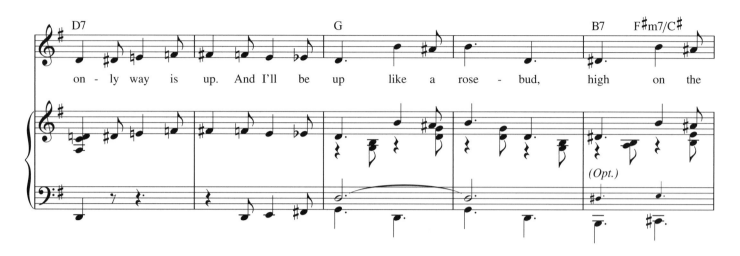

on - ly way is up. And I'll be up like a rose - bud, high on the

vine; don't thumb your nose, bud, take a tip from mine. I'm a

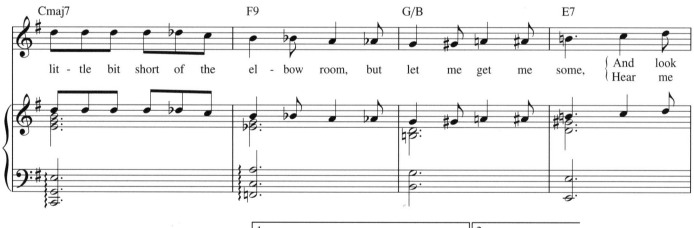

lit - tle bit short of the el - bow room, but let me get me some, { And look / Hear me

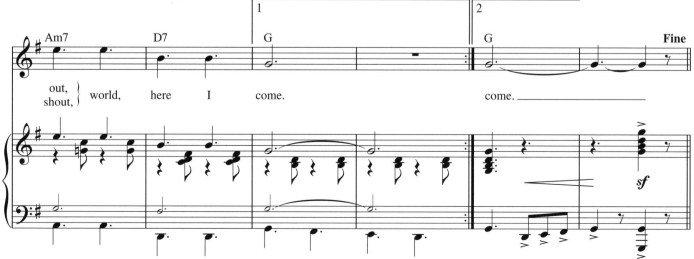

out, / shout, } world, here I come.   come.

Interlude (ad lib.)

No - bod - y in the world was ev - er with - out a pray'r;

how can you win the world, if no - bod - y knows you're there.

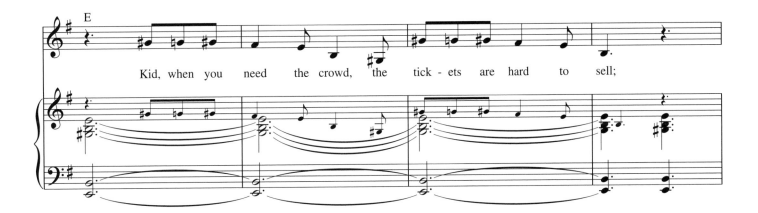

Kid, when you need the crowd, the tick - ets are hard to sell;

D.S. al Fine

still you can lead the crowd, if you can get up and yell:

I Could Write A Book

from PAL JOEY
Words by Lorenz Hart
Music by Richard Rodgers

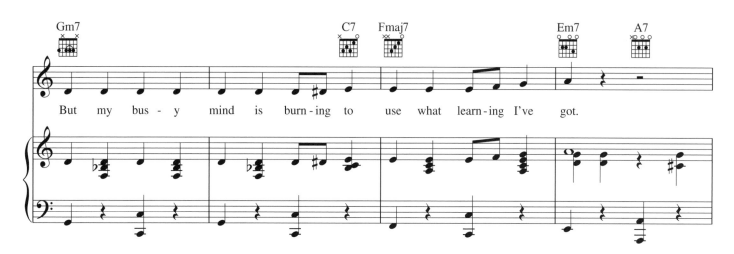

But my bus-y mind is burn-ing to use what learn-ing I've got.

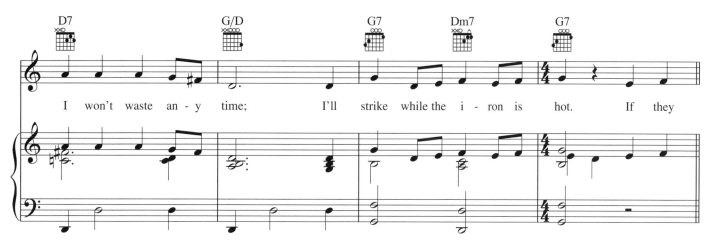

I won't waste an-y time; I'll strike while the i-ron is hot. If they

asked me, I could write a book _____ a-bout the

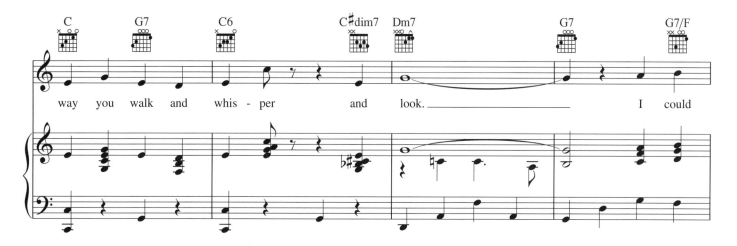

way you walk and whis-per and look. _____ I could

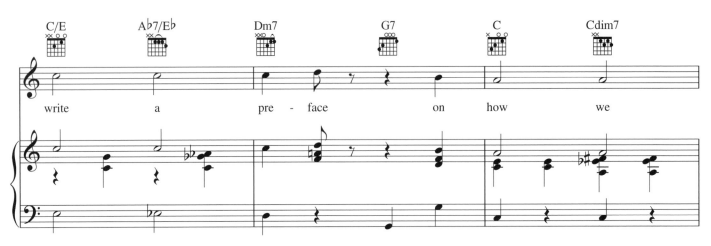

write a pre - face on how we

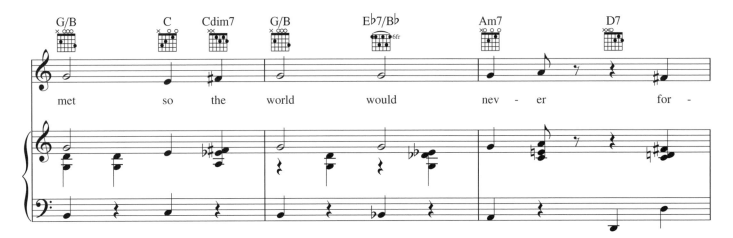

met so the world would nev - er for -

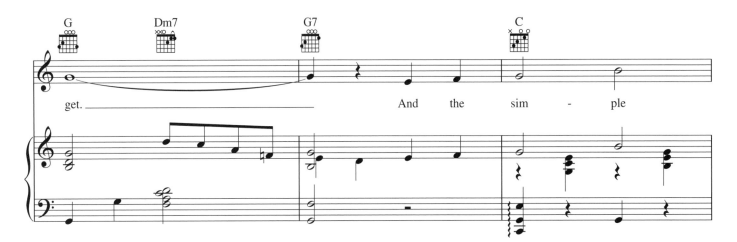

get. And the sim - ple

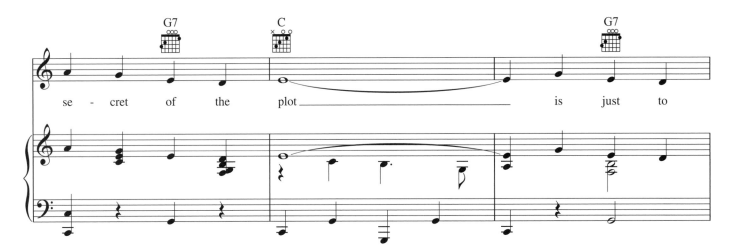

se - cret of the plot is just to

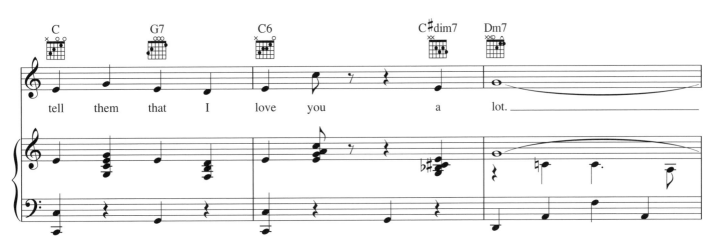

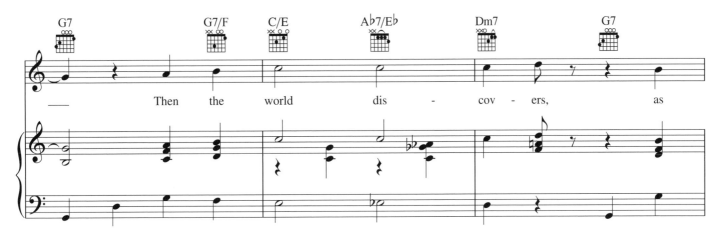

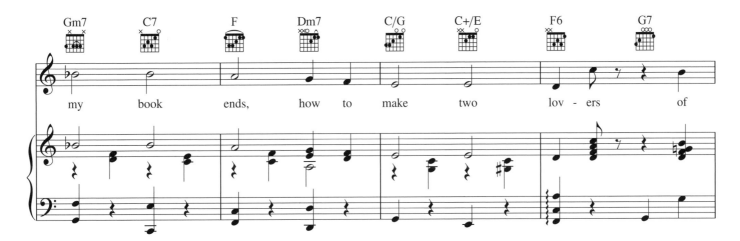

I Dreamed A Dream

from LES MISÉRABLES
Music by Claude-Michel Schönberg
Lyrics by Alain Boublil, Jean-Marc Natel and Herbert Kretzmer

paid,   no song un -sung, no wine un - tast - ed.

But   the ti - gers come at   night   with their voic - es soft as

poco più mosso

thun - der,   as   they tear   your hope a - part,

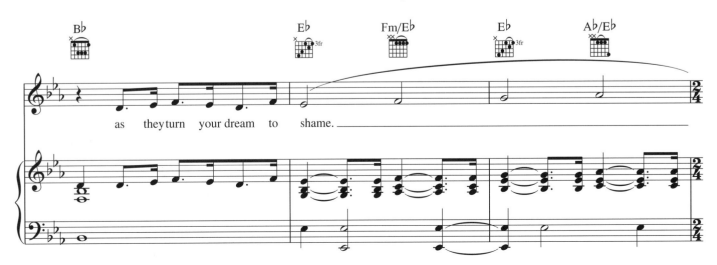

as   they turn your dream to   shame. _____

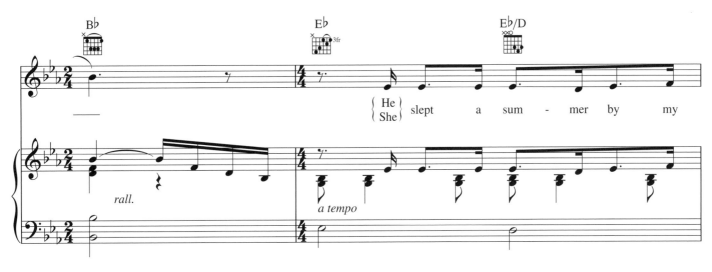

He / She slept a sum-mer by my

side. He / She filled my days with end-less won-der.

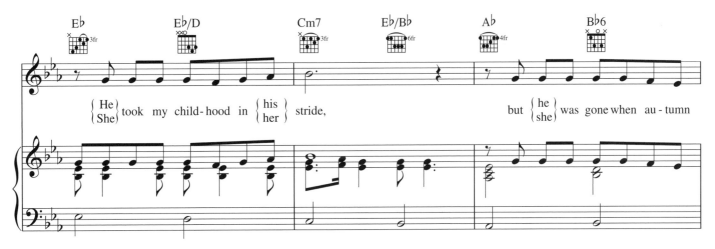

He / She took my child-hood in his / her stride, but he / she was gone when au-tumn

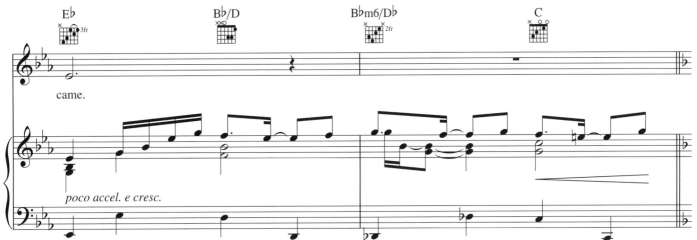

came.

poco accel. e cresc.

be so dif - f'rent from this hell I'm

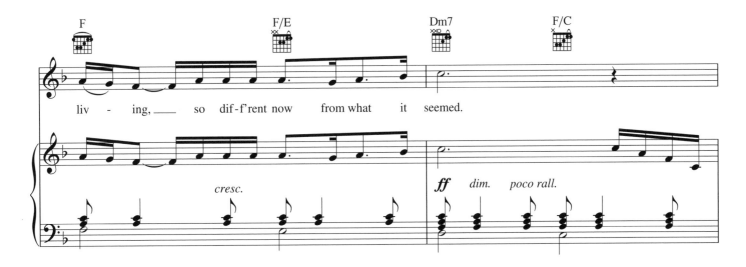

liv - ing, ___ so dif-f'rent now from what it seemed.

Now life has killed the dream I dreamed.

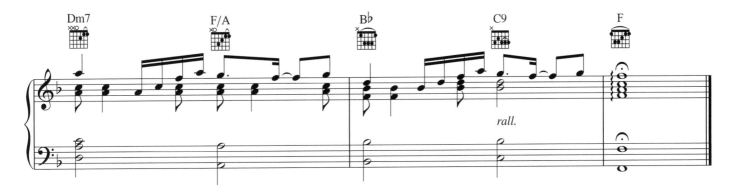

I'll Never Fall In Love Again

from PROMISES, PROMISES
Lyric by Hal David
Music by Burt Bacharach

Rhythmically

What do you get when you fall in love? ___ A {girl}{guy} with a pin to burst ___

___ your bub - ble. That's what you get for all your trou - ble!

I'll nev - er fall in love a - gain. ___

What do you get when you kiss a {girl? / guy?} You get e-nough germs to catch __
What do you get when you give your heart? __ You get it all bro-ken up __
What do you get when you need a {girl? / guy?} You get e-nough tears to fill __

__ pneu-mo-nia. Af-ter you do, {she'll / he'll} nev-er phone __ you.
__ and bat-tered. That's what you get, a heart that's shat-tered.
__ an o-cean. That's what you get for your de-vo-tion.

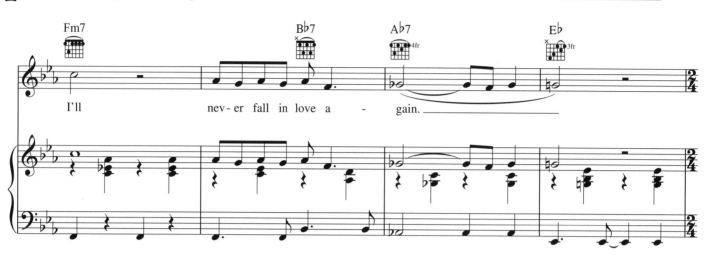

I'll   nev - er fall in love a - gain. _____

I'll   nev - er fall in love a - gain. _____

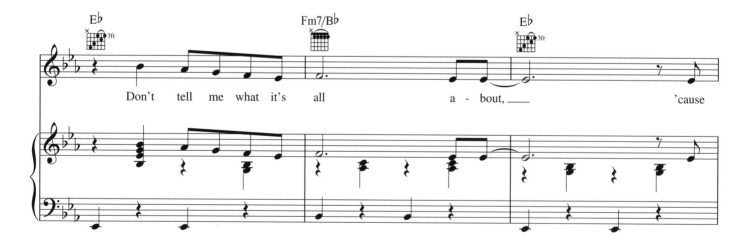

Don't tell me what it's all   a - bout, _____   'cause

I've been there __ and I'm   glad I'm out. _____   Out of those chains, those

chains that bind __ you, that is why I'm here to re-mind you.

What do you get when you fall in love? __ You on-ly get lies and pain __

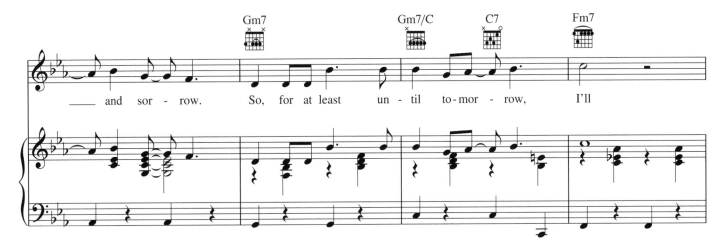

__ and sor - row. So, for at least un - til to-mor - row, I'll

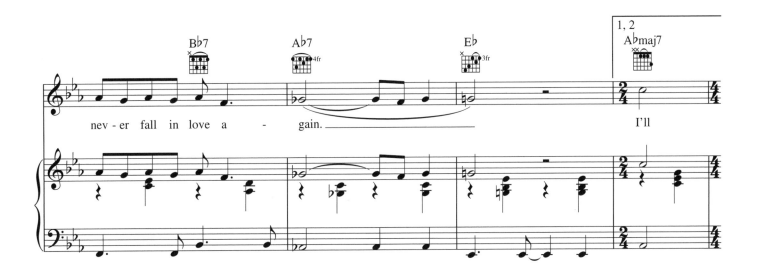

nev - er fall in love a - gain. _____ I'll

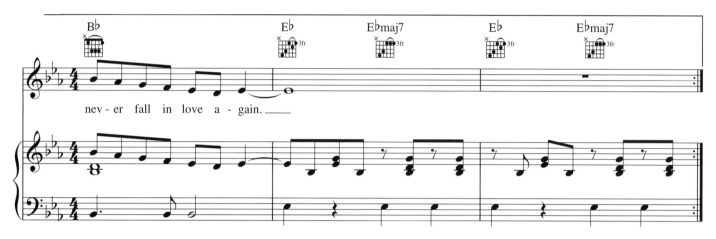

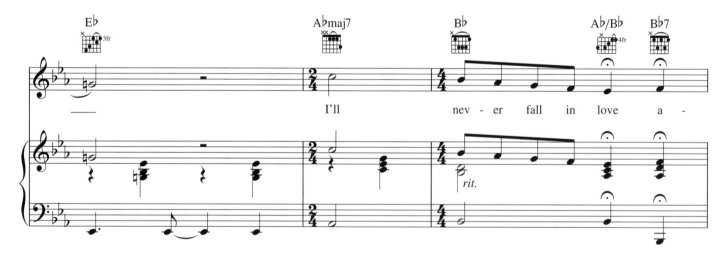

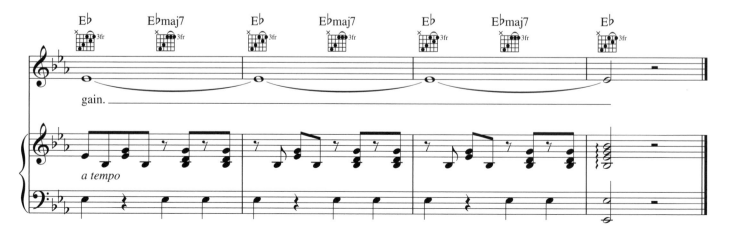

Let's Hang On

featured in JERSEY BOYS
Words and Music by Bob Crewe, Denny Randell and Sandy Linzer

to what we've got. Don't let go, ____ girl, we've got a ____

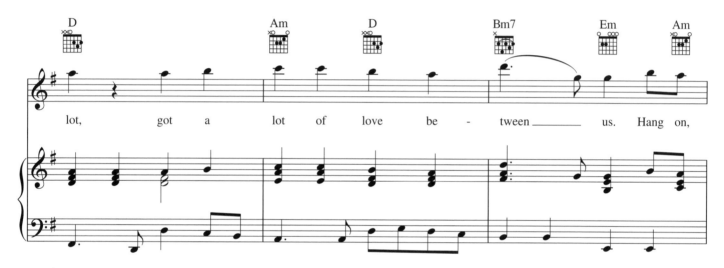

lot, got a lot of love be - tween ____ us. Hang on,

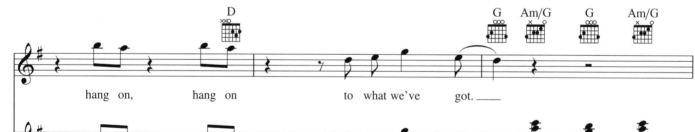

hang on, hang on to what we've got. ____

You say you're gon - na go and call ____ it quits, ____ gon - na
There is - n't an - y - thing I would - n't ____ do, ____ I'd pay

chuck it all ___ and break our love ___ to bits. (Break-in' up.) ___ I ___ wish ___ you'd
an - y price ___ to get in good ___ with you. (Patch it up.) ___ Give ___ me ___ a

nev - er said it. No, ___ no, ___ we'll both re - gret it.
sec - ond turn in. Don't ___ cool ___ off while I'm burn - in'.

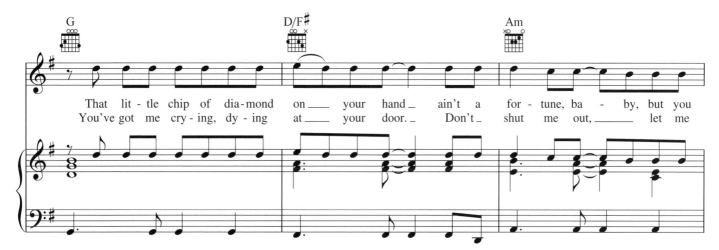

That lit - tle chip of dia-mond on ___ your hand ___ ain't a for - tune, ba - by, but you
You've got me cry - ing, dy - ing at ___ your door. ___ Don't ___ shut me out, ___ let me

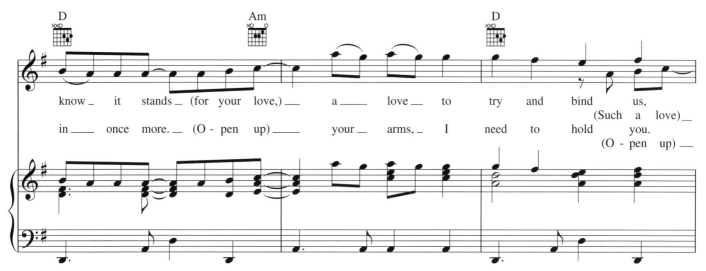

know ___ it stands ___ (for your love,) ___ a ___ love ___ to try and bind us,
in ___ once more. (O - pen up) ___ your ___ arms, ___ I need to hold you.
(Such a love) _
(O - pen up) _

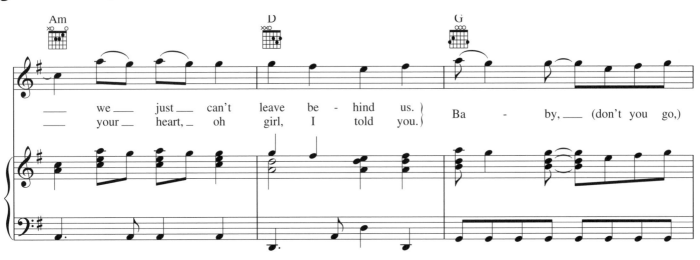

we ___ just ___ can't leave be - hind us. }
your ___ heart, ___ oh girl, I told you. } Ba - by, ___ (don't you go,)

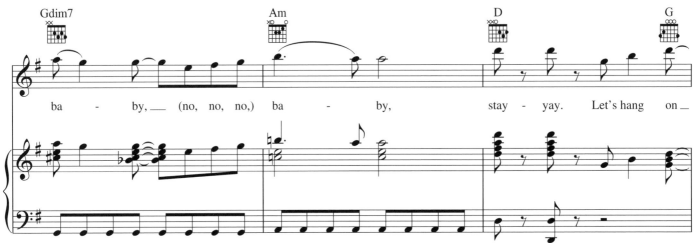

ba - by, ___ (no, no, no,) ba - by, stay - yay. Let's hang on ___

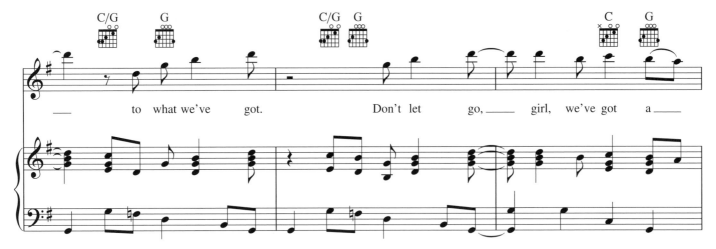

___ to what we've got. Don't let go, ___ girl, we've got a ___

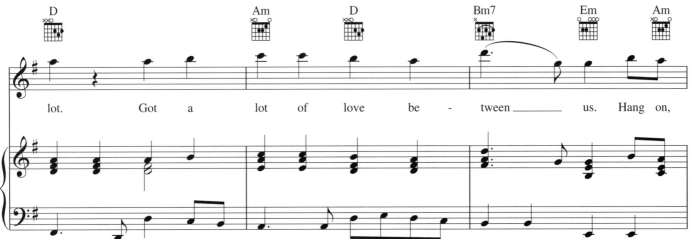

lot. Got a lot of love be - tween ___ us. Hang on,

hang on,   hang on   to what we've   got. ____

(Fade 2nd time)

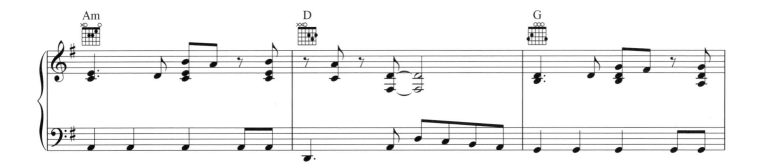

Optional Ending

If I Loved You

from CAROUSEL

Lyrics by Oscar Hammerstein II
Music by Richard Rodgers

Allegretto moderato

JULIE: When I worked in the mill,
BILLY: Kind - a scraw - ny and pale,

Weav - in' at the loom,
Pick - in' at my food

I'd gaze ab - sent -
And love - sick like

mind - ed at the roof _____
an - y oth - er guy _____

And half the time the shut - tle 'd
I'd throw a - way my sweat - er and

tan - gle in the threads,
dress up like a dude

And the warp 'd get mixed with the woof _____
in a dick - ey and a col - lar and a tie _____

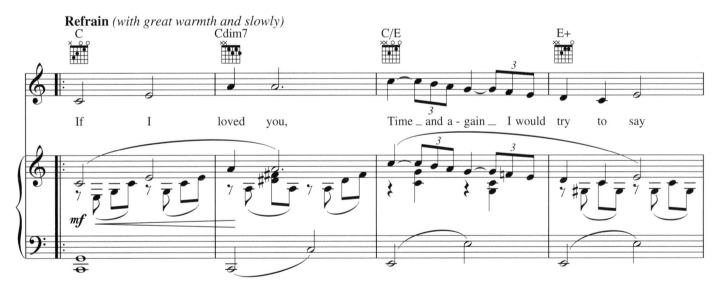

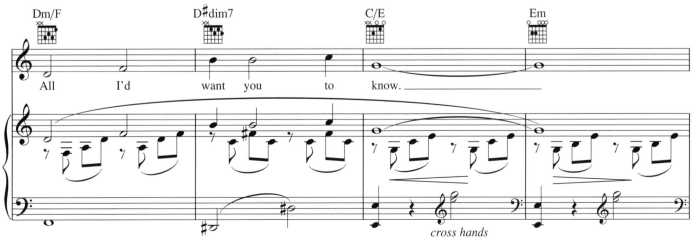

cross hands

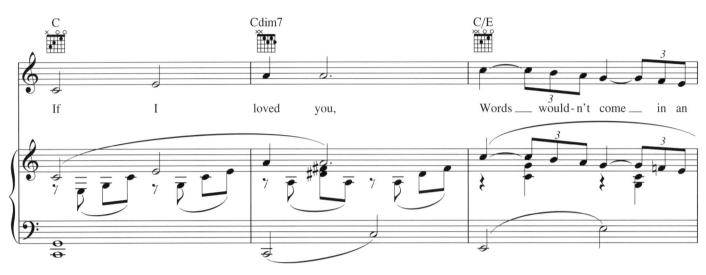

If I loved you, Words__ would-n't come__ in an

eas - y way, 'Round in cir - cles I'd go.__

Long - in' to tell you, but a - fraid and

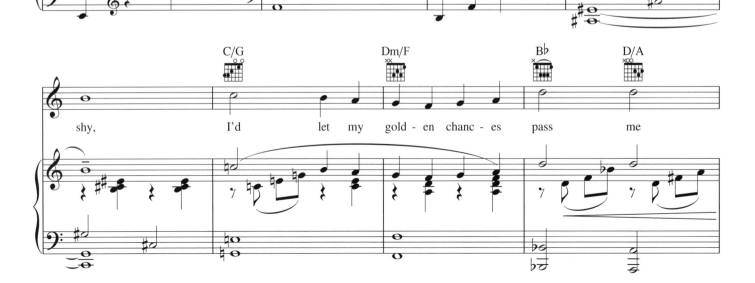

shy, I'd let my gold - en chanc - es pass me

by! Soon you'd leave me, off ___ you would go ___ in the

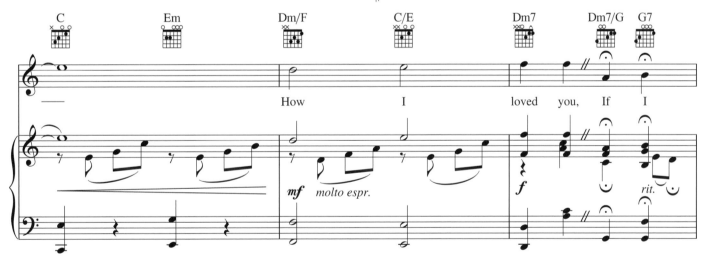

mist of day, Nev - er, nev - er to know ___

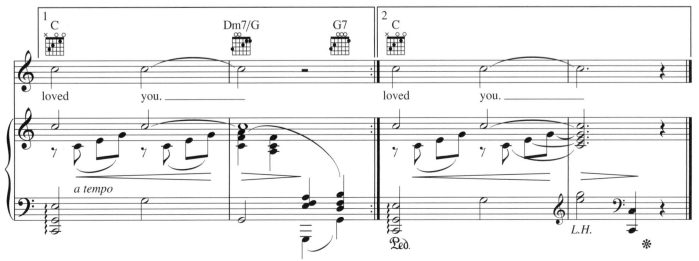

How I loved you, If I loved you. ___ loved you. ___

It's A Grand Night For Singing

from STATE FAIR

Lyrics by Oscar Hammerstein II
Music by Richard Rodgers

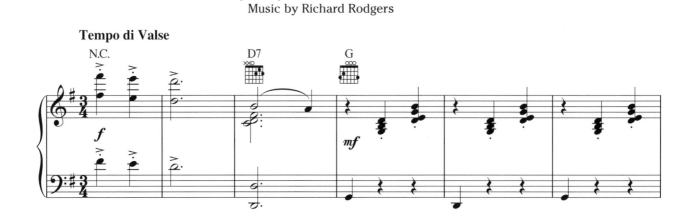

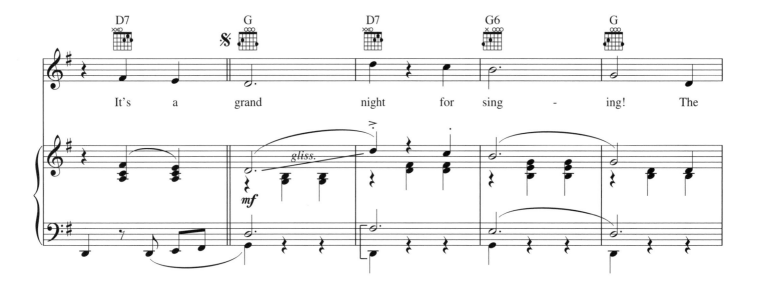

It's a grand night for sing - ing! The

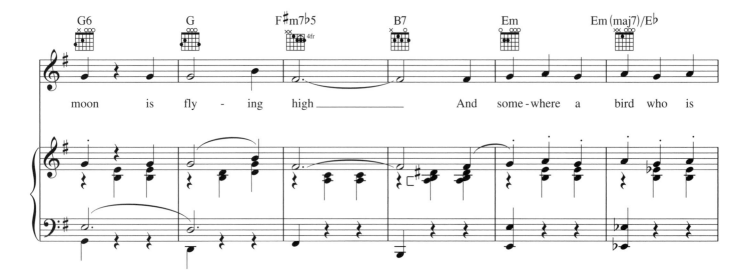

moon is fly - ing high _____ And some - where a bird who is

bound he'll be heard, Is throw - ing his heart at the sky.

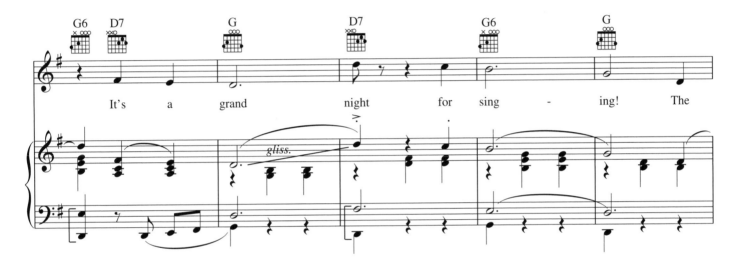

It's a grand night for sing - ing! The

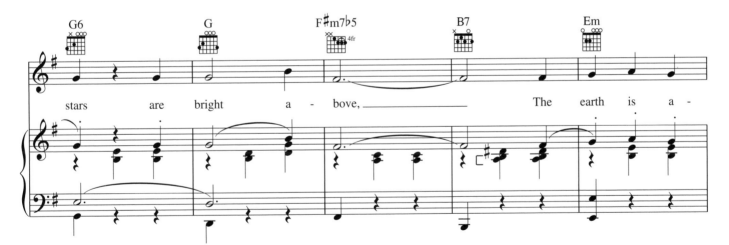

stars are bright a - bove, _____ The earth is a -

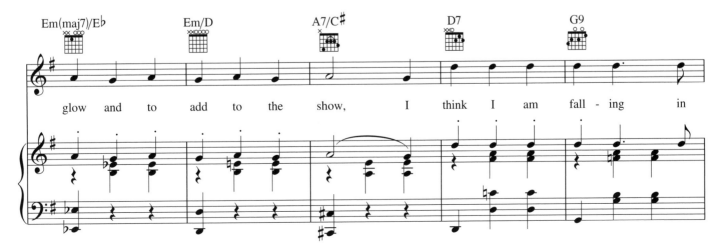

glow and to add to the show, I think I am fall - ing in

love. _____ Fall - ing, Fall -

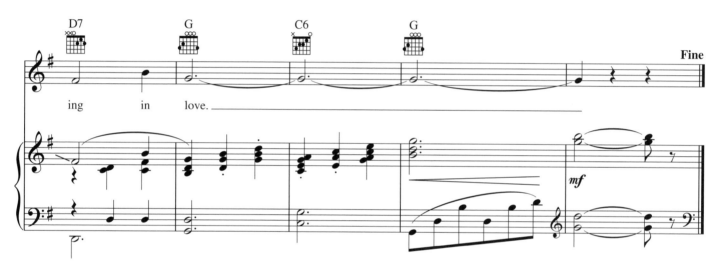

ing in love. _____

Fine

Interlude

May - be it's more than the

moon, _____ May - be it's more than the birds. _____

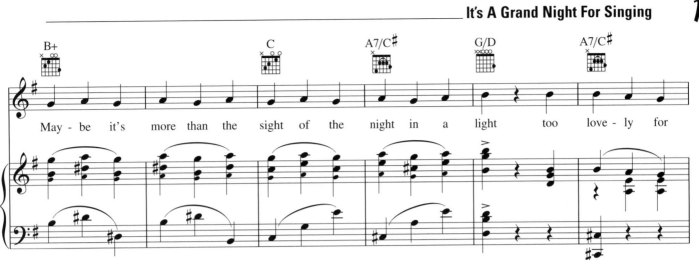

May - be it's more than the sight of the night in a light too love - ly for

words. _____ May - be it's more than the earth _____

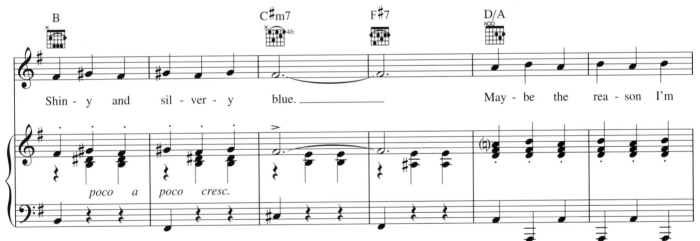

Shin - y and sil - ver - y blue. _____ May - be the rea - son I'm

poco a poco cresc.

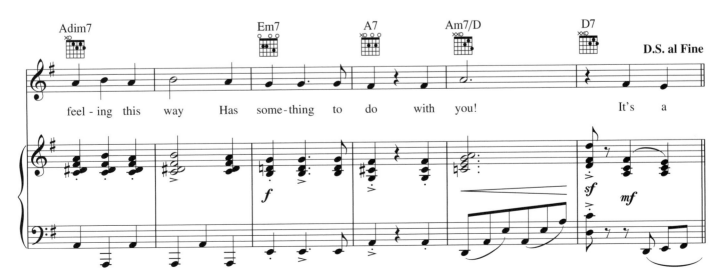

D.S. al Fine

feel - ing this way Has some - thing to do with you! It's a

f   *sf*   *mf*

The Lady Is A Tramp

from BABES IN ARMS
Words by Lorenz Hart
Music by Richard Rodgers

both - er   with   peo - ple I   hate, _____

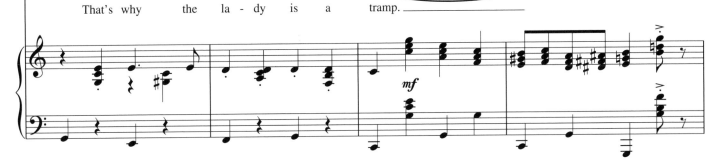

That's why   the   la - dy   is a   tramp. _____

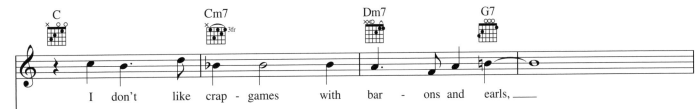

I   don't   like   crap - games   with   bar - ons and   earls, _____

Won't go   to   Har - lem   in   er - mine and   pearls. _____

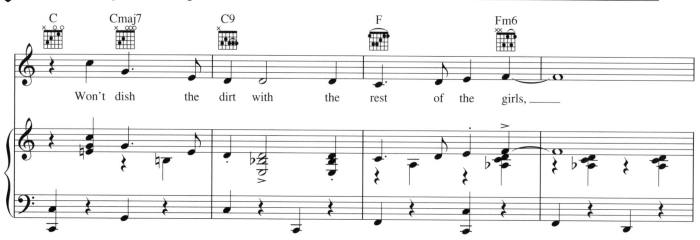

Won't dish the dirt with the rest of the girls, _____

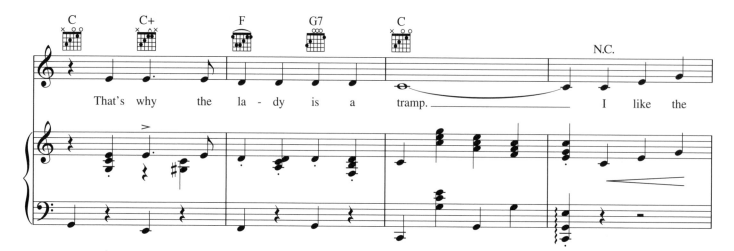

That's why the la-dy is a tramp. _____ I like the

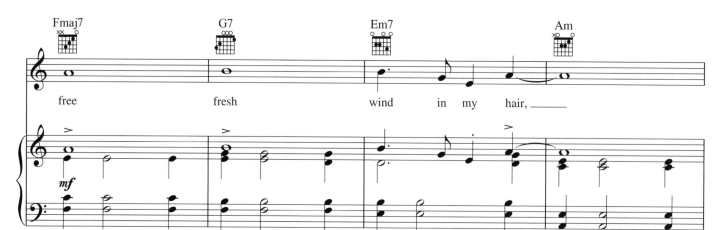

free   fresh   wind in my hair, _____

Life with-out care. _____ I'm broke, _ it's oke. _

Hate Cal - i - for - nia, It's cold and it's damp, ___

That's why the la - dy is a tramp. ___

la - dy is a tramp. ___

Performance Notes

All I Ask of You (page 7)

Inspired by an earlier musical based on the Gaston Leroux novel of the same name, *The Phantom of the Opera* was written by Andrew Lloyd Webber, with lyrics by Charles Hart, and additional lyrics by Richard Stilgoe. Webber's original production was directed by Harold Prince and choreographed by Gillian Lynne, and starred Michael Crawford (the Phantom), Sarah Brightman (Christine Daaé), and Steve Barton (Raoul, the Vicomte de Chagny). *Phantom* opened on October 9, 1986 and, despite some early negative reviews, now holds the record as the longest-running Broadway musical ever.

The show tells the story of a gorgeous singer, Christine Daaé, and the Phantom, a shadowy, deformed musical prodigy who spends his time obsessing over her and terrorizing the Paris Opéra Populaire. "All I Ask of You" is sung at the end of Act I after Raoul, the Vicomte de Chagny, a patron of the Opéra Populaire and a childhood love of Christine's, has reunited with her. Christine tells Raoul that she has encountered the Phantom, and Raoul, though a bit skeptical about her claim, joins her in a lovely duet in which he pledges to cherish and protect her always. The eavesdropping Phantom, heartbroken but hardly vanquished, follows with a malevolent reprise of "All I Ask of You."

Don't be intimidated by the tricky-looking key of D♭ major (five flats). Just take the time to slowly and deliberately get "All I Ask of You" under your fingers, one measure at a time. Speaking of flats, note the inclusion of the note C♭ throughout. It is *enharmonic* to, or the same as, the note B. Also note that the C♭ chord is foreign to the key of D♭. Listen to the soulful quality this *outside* chord provides.

The song has some rhythms that might prove problematic. If you find yourself getting tripped up on those 16th-note syncopations, just isolate each troublesome spot and practice it over and over again until you can play it smoothly.

 Look out for those sneaky changes in meter. Here and there, the song moves from 4/4 to 2/4 to 3/4 over the course of three bars, so be sure to drop the appropriate number of beats without letting the basic pulse slip. Use a metronome if necessary.

Always Look on the Bright Side of Life (page 12)

Based on the hit comedy film *Monty Python and the Holy Grail* (1975), *Spamalot* sends up both the Arthurian legend and Broadway theater. The book and lyrics were written by Python alumnus Eric Idle, and John Du Prez composed the music. *Spamalot* recreates on stage many of the comic bits that helped the film achieve its iconic status: legless knights, men in tights, and murderous rabbits. Directed by Mike Nichols and choreographed by Casey Nicholaw, the musical opened on March 17, 2005, with a cast that included such stars as David Hyde Pierce, Tim Curry, and Hank Azaria. It was a success before it even opened — revenue from advance sales were reported at $18 million, a Broadway box-office record. The show itself was a commercial and critical smash, winning three Tony Awards, including Best Musical of the 2004–2005 season, and it continues to kill on Broadway.

Written by Idle, reportedly as a spoof of a Disney song, "Always Look on the Bright Side of Life" is actually borrowed from Monty Python's *Life of Brian* (1979). Over the years, it has become a singalong favorite at football games and other sporting events.

The disarmingly cheerful tune is sung in Act II, then again during the curtain call. It kicks off here in the key of A major with a I–vi–ii–V progression (A–F♯m–Bm7–E9) propelling the verse. Throughout, be sure to include the whistle — contributed by Idle's collaborator Neil Innes, this part really makes the song.

Also look out for the song's *modulations,* or changes of key. Although the new key signature may appear difficult, the underlying progression doesn't change. That I–v—ii–V progression is still there! In the bar after the second ending, for instance, the tune keeps the same basic progression but is moved up a half step, to the key of B♭ major, then 16 measures later, up an additional half step, to B major.

Be careful to transition smoothly between these sections and don't let them trip your fingers up. Taking the time to learn the song slowly, one bar, one phrase, or one section at a time, can help ensure that you're able to play the transitions, and the whole song, without stumbling.

Another Op'nin', Another Show (page 19)

In 1937, the great American songwriter Cole Porter — the celebrated composer of "What Is This Thing Called Love," "I Get a Kick Out of You," "Night and Day," and countless other songs — was seriously injured in a horseback-riding accident. For a time afterwards his work lost something in commercial appeal, but Porter once again enjoyed smashing success with his musical *Kiss Me, Kate,* which in 1949 won the first Tony Award for Best Musical. Fifty years later, a revival won the same Tony.

Featuring a book by Samuel and Bella Spewack, *Kiss Me, Kate* employs a play within a play as its central plot point. A group of romantically mismatched actors, with the help of some gullible gangsters, combine to stage William Shakespeare's *The Taming of the Shrew.* The original production opened on December 30, 1948 and, in a record for a Porter vehicle, ran for 1,077 performances. Directed by John C. Wilson and choreographed by Hanya Holmthe, the musical boasted a cast that included Alfred Drake, Patricia Morison, Lisa Kirk, and Harold Lang. "Another Op'nin', Another Show," the musical's opening number, is a rollicking tune that perfectly captures the excitement and anxiety experienced by everyone associated with a play on opening night in a big city.

In the music, notice the time signature — a c with a vertical line through it, representing *cut time,* or 2/2. To most effectively convey this bouncy feel, look out for the bass notes and make sure they only sound on beats 1 and 2, except where otherwise notated.

Look out for the numerous expressive markings. Seen in the first full bar, for example, are *staccato* signs (those dots below noteheads) — cut those notes short. In the third bar, there is an accent mark (>) — play those notes louder. In the second bar, you find a combination accent mark/staccato — you guessed it, play the notes both shorter and louder.

Beware of the 16th-note *grace notes* throughout. In bar 17, for example, rapidly play the notes B, C, and D immediately before the first beat without losing the time. If doing so is too difficult at first, just learn the song without the grace notes and add them later. Also notice the multiple endings, which you find throughout this book. Play the whole song up to the bracketed first ending, and when you get to the backwards repeat sign, go back to the forward-facing repeat sign and play everything again, skipping over the first ending and finishing the song with the second.

Any Dream Will Do (page 24)

Based on the Biblical story of Joseph, *Joseph and the Amazing Technicolor Dreamcoat* was the second musical written by Andrew Lloyd Webber and Tim Rice, and the first they produced. The show was commissioned by London's Colet Court preparatory school, and the original production, which made its debut on March 1, 1968, included student performers and was only 15 minutes long. The show in its current form was staged by assorted amateur and professional groups throughout the 1970s and was recorded by Decca Records. It wasn't until January 27, 1982 that it hit Broadway, running for 749 performances. With its appealing mix of musical styles — rock, country, and disco, among others — and universal themes, *Joseph* went on to become one of the most popular and profitable musicals of all time. In Act I, "Any Dream Will Do" is sung by the narrator, telling the story of Joseph to a group of children, encouraging them to become dreamers.

The song is in the key of C major and kicks off with a I–IV–I–V progression (C–F/C–C–G6), built on the first, fourth, and fifth notes of the C major scale. Note the use of *pedal point,* or a constant bass note. The root of the C chord (C) is placed beneath the F chord, forming a 2nd-inversion triad (F/C). Also observe that over the G chord, the melody note E forms a G6 chord (G–B–D–E) in the midst of otherwise *triadic* (three-note) harmony. The verses are also built from I, IV, and V chords, and one new sound is introduced — the dominant 7th chord, G7 (G–B–D–F), formed by adding the ♭7 (F) to the V chord.

Starting on the IV chord, the bridge is a bit more harmonically complex. The first two measures have three different types of F chords: F (F–A–C), F6 (F–A–C–D), and Fmaj7 (F–A–C–E). And beginning with the lyric "colours," you see more pedal point as C, G7, Dm, and D7 chords are all placed over a G bass note. Take the time to get these swiftly moving changes securely under your fingers, and pay close attention to how each chord sounds over the pedal. In conjunction with the lyric "May I return," a G7 chord neatly resolves to a C chord for the final verse.

As Long as He Needs Me (page 34)

The first successful musical adaptation of a Charles Dickens novel, *Oliver!,* featuring words and music by Lionel Bart, recounts the travails of a young orphan in Victorian England. The original London production opened on June 30, 1960, featuring a unique revolving set and a cast that included Ron Moody (Fagin), Georgia Brown (Nancy), and Barry Humphries (Mr. Sowerberry). A long run helped launch the careers of two childhood actors who later became rock stars: Davy Jones (The Monkees) and Phil Collins. *Oliver!* first hit Broadway on January 6, 1963 and later enjoyed revivals in New York, in 1984, as well as in London, in 1994.

"As Long as He Needs Me" is first sung in Act II by Nancy, a prostitute who develops a motherly affection for Oliver. In the song, Nancy expresses devotion to her hooligan boyfriend, Bill Sykes, despite his mistreatment of her. As a reprise near the end of the show, the song changes its tenor a bit when Nancy uses it to express her affection for Oliver.

The music to "As Long as He Needs Me" features plenty of *accidentals* — sharps and flats not found in the song's key of C major — so try learning the right- and left-hand parts separately and then combine them.

The music contains a couple of symbols that may be unfamiliar to you. In the second and final bars are *fermata* signs — dots enclosed by a semicircle — which instruct the player to extend notes as long as he wishes, in an unmeasured fashion. In the penultimate measure, between the treble and bass staves are *crescendo* marks, which indicate that you should gradually increase the volume until you reach *forte (f)*, or "loud," in the last bar.

Big Spender (page 31)

Adapted from the 1957 Federico Fellini film *Nights of Cabiria,* the musical *Sweet Charity* features music by Cy Coleman, lyrics by Dorothy Fields, and a book by Neil Simon. Set in 1960s New York City (whereas Fellini's film takes place in Italy), this delightfully fun musical centers around the misadventures of Charity Agnes Valentine, a dancehall hostess at the Fandango Ballroom who has a bad habit of giving both her heart and money to the wrong sort of guy. The original Broadway production, which opened January 29, 1966, was directed and choreographed by Bob Fosse and starred Gwen Verdon in the title role, with a cast that featured John McMartin, Helen Gallagher, Thelma Oliver, and James Luisi. It was nominated for 12 Tony Awards, winning one for Fosse's choreography.

A 1986 revival of *Sweet Charity,* starring Debbie Allen, Bebe Neuwirth, and Michael Rupert, won four Tony Awards and ran for 369 performances. A second revival in 1995, starring Christina Applegate, Denis O'Hare, and Ernie Sabella, ran for 279 performances and was nominated for three Tony Awards.

"Big Spender," the show's most popular tune, is delivered in Act I by the hostesses of the Fandango Ballroom. A wide variety of artists have covered the song, including Shirley Bassey, Peggy Lee, and the rock band Queen.

Take note of the song's "roadmap." When you get to the indication *D.S. al Coda* (*dal segno al coda,* meaning "from the sign to the coda"), find the sign at the beginning of the fifth measure. Start there, and play until you get to the indication *To Coda,* where you'll skip to the indented system marked *Coda* and proceed with rest of the piece.

Cabaret (page 36)

First produced on Broadway on November 20, 1966, *Cabaret* (which was originally titled *Welcome to Berlin*), featured a book by Joe Masteroff, lyrics by Fred Ebb, and music by John Kander. The musical is based on the John Van Druten play *I Am a Camera,* which itself was adapted from the novel *Mr. Norris Changes Trains* and the short-story collection *Goodbye to Berlin,* both by Christopher Isherwood. The original production of this enormous hit — it ran for 1,165 performances — was directed by Hal Prince and choreographed by Ron Field. An early cast featured Jill Haworth (Sally), Bert Convy (Cliff), Lotte Lenya (Fräulein Schneider), Jack Gilford (Herr Schultz), and Joel Grey (the Emcee).

Set in a seedy Berlin nightspot, the Kit Kat Klub, at the time of the Nazis' rise to power, the show focuses on the relationship between a young cabaret performer, Sally Bowles, and an American writer, Cliff Bradshaw. A subplot explores another romance, between a German boardinghouse owner, Fräulein Schneider, and a Jewish fruit seller, Herr Schultz. Meanwhile, the show is presided over by the club's master of ceremonies, the Emcee, through whose eyes the story unfolds. The song "Cabaret," belted out by Sally, comes at the end of Act II, just before the finale.

The song makes use of some rather sophisticated harmonies in the key of E♭ major. In the first bar, for example, there is an E♭maj9 chord, which is built by adding the 9th (F) to an E♭maj7 chord (E♭–G–B♭–D). In the next measure is a B♭7♯5(♭9), a tense-sounding chord constructed by raising the 5th of a B♭7 chord (B♭–D–F–A♭) by a half step, to F♯, and adding the ♭9 (C♭). Familiarize yourself with these chords, because they appear in countless songs.

The E♭(add9) in the verse is simply an E♭ major triad (E♭–G–B♭) with a 9th on top. Notice the nice half-step movement between the 9th of E♭(add9) and the ♯5 (F♯) of B♭7♯5, a favorite of jazz musicians. Also, check out the use of the I7 (dominant) chord in the seventh and eighth measures of this section, in which the flatted 7th (D) lends a particularly bluesy feel to the proceedings. Then, at the end of the verse (first ending, second bar) there appears one of the most common progressions in jazz, the ii–V (Fm7–B♭9), which smoothly sets up a return to the I chord (E♭[add9]) at the top of the verse.

Camelot *(page 40)*

Lyricist Alan Jay Lerner and composer Frederick Loewe followed up on their monster 1959 hit *My Fair Lady* with *Camelot,* an adaptation of *The Once and Future King,* T.H. White's novel based on the legend of King Arthur and the Knights of the Round Table. *Camelot* tells the story of an affair between Guenevere, King Arthur's wife and Queen, and his friend Sir Lancelot. The original production was directed by Moss Hart and starred Richard Burton as King Arthur, Julie Andrews as Guenevere, and Robert Goulet as Sir Lancelot. When it first opened in Toronto, the show was quite long, leaving audiences so exhausted that it became clear to all involved that a major edit was necessary. By the time it hit Broadway, on December 3, 1960, the musical had been shortened by about 90 minutes and this did the trick — *Camelot* won four Tony Awards and enjoyed an 873-performance run. In the song "Camelot," sung early in Act I, Arthur extols the virtues of his domain to the maiden Guenevere, thereby convincing her to be his bride.

Kicking off in the key of F major, "Camelot" features some harmony that can be described as *static,* or slow-moving. For example, the first eight bars of the verse are essentially one big I chord, F, spelled F–A–C, with the 6th (D, forming F6) and 7th (E, Fmaj7) added here and there to add a little harmonic variety. Note the subtly different qualities of these chords. The V chord (C7) then appears for four measures, embellished by diminished 7th chords. Note that D♯dim7 (D♯–F♯–A–C) is actually a reordering of the notes of F♯dim7 (F♯–A–C–E♭[D♯]).

In the thirty-third full measure of the piece comes a harmonic surprise, seemingly out of nowhere — an A chord that serves as a V chord, setting up a temporary visit, beginning in bar 37, to the key of D major. Whereas previously the F chord was embellished with notes above the triad, here the D chord is played against an invigorating moving bass line below, comprised of the notes C♯, B, and A. This arrangement continues into bar 45, which also sees the return of the original key, F. After you have a handle on all the harmonic moves, work the song up into a sprightly vibe.

Can You Feel the Love Tonight *(page 46)*

The Lion King, based on the 1994 animated Disney film of the same name, features music by Elton John and lyrics by Tim Rice. The musical is the story of a young lion prince, Simba, heir to the throne of his father, King Mufasa. The king's brother Scar, who is next in the line of ascension, orchestrates a stampede that kills Mufasa and then tricks Simba, his nephew, into taking the blame. Simba flees the kingdom in shame, leaving Scar as king, but he later returns to claim what is rightfully his. "Can You Feel the Love Tonight," which won an Oscar for Best Song for the Disney film, is the highlight of a tender scene between Simba and his childhood friend Nala.

Directed by Julie Taymor, the original production of *The Lion King* was staged with the actors in animal costumes and giant puppets. In October of 1997 it debuted on Broadway, where it was an instant success, and won a Tony for Best Musical. The musical is still running — a version touring the United States is similar to the Broadway production, but the elaborate scenery that emerges from the stage floor, including grasslands and a stampede, has been scaled back for logistical reasons.

The piano part mirrors the vocal melody, fleshing things out with chords and fills, the latter of which tend to fall on beat 4. If the fills, with all those 16th notes, give you any trouble, omit them when first learning the song and concentrate on them separately. When taking this approach, hold the dotted-eighth through the end of bar 5.

To capture the song's tender vibe, be sure to carefully observe the expressive markings. As directed at the beginning of the song, depress the sustain pedal liberally throughout, lifting when the chords change, and play everything *legato* — smooth and flowing, without pauses between the notes. At the end of the 12th bar, notice the direction *poco cresc. (crescendo),* which directs you to raise the volume a little. The *poco dim. (diminuendo)* before the first ending is a suggestion to play a bit more softly.

Two tempo markings are found in the final system of the song — *rall. (rallentando)* means to gradually play more slowly, and *molto rit. (ritardando)* means to play much slower. The squiggly vertical line in the final bar indicates that you should roll the chord from the lowest note to the highest.

Don't Cry for Me Argentina *(page 50)*

Written by Andrew Lloyd Webber and Tim Rice, Evita is based on the story of Eva Perón, who as the second wife of the President of Argentina, Juan Perón, came to share power with him. The main source of the musical was the Mary Main biography *Evita: The Woman with the Whip.* The musical began its life in 1976 as an album, with the lead role sung by Julie Covington. It was subsequently retooled — songs and lyrics were dropped, added, and changed — before it opened on London's West End in 1978, and then on Broadway the following year.

The original London production, which ran for 2,900 performances, was directed by Harold Prince, choreographed by Larry Fuller, and produced by Robert Stigwood. The cast included Elaine Paige in the lead role, Joss Ackland as Perón, and David Essex as the revolutionary leader Che Guevara. The first Broadway production featured Patti LuPone as Evita, Bob Gunton as Perón, and Mandy Patinkin as Che, and ran for 1,567 performances. In 1996 *Evita* was made into a film starring Madonna in the title role, Jonathan Pryce as Perón, and Antonio Banderas as Che.

Early in Act II Evita sings "Don't Cry for Me Argentina" to her supporters. This beautiful tune is in the somewhat difficult key of D♭ major, so look out for all those flats. "Don't Cry" makes extensive use of a pedal tone, with the I (D♭), IV (G♭), V (A♭7), vi (B♭m) and II (E♭m) chords all played above a D bass note. Play through the 15-bar introduction slowly, really soaking in the unique sounds created by the nearly constant D♭. For good measure, try playing other chords above the note. Another noteworthy device in the arrangement is the use of suspended chords. In bar 7, for example, the D♭sus chord substitutes a D♭ triad's 4th (G♭) for the 3rd (F). This creates tension, which is resolved by moving down to the 3rd in that same measure.

Running throughout the song is a rhythm that may be unfamiliar to you — the quarter-note triplet, or three quarter notes in the space usually occupied by two. To feel this rhythm, try counting eighth note triplets on each beat: "trip-uh-let, trip-uh-let," and so on. In the span of two beats, a quarter note will then fall on the first "trip," the first "let," and the second "uh." If this rhythm is giving you trouble, count and practice it extremely slowly until you feel it in your gut — and your fingers.

Everything's Alright *(page 58)*

More a rock opera than a musical, *Jesus Christ Superstar* was written by Tim Rice and Andrew Lloyd Webber. The story deals with the conflicts between Jesus and Judas Iscariot as seen through the eyes of Judas. The action takes place during the last seven days of Jesus's life, from his arrival in Jerusalem until the Crucifixion. The use of slang and references to pop culture lend a modern feel to the proceedings. As with other Andrew Lloyd Webber productions, *Jesus* started as an album, released in 1970. The first U.S. production was staged, in June of 1971, by high school actors in Southold, New York.

The Broadway production, directed by Tom O'Horgan and starring Jeff Fenholt, Ben Vereen, and Bob Bingham, opened October 12, 1971 and ran for 711 performances. In 1972, *Jesus* picked up five Tony Award nominations, and it subsequently went on to become a cultural phenomenon, with performances staged in India, Bulgaria, Russia, and other locales far from the Great White Way.

With "Everything's All Right" Mary Magdalene tries to reassure Jesus and relax him with ointment. The song is reprised later in the first act, when Mary finds Jesus disturbed after his encounter with a mob of lepers. The tune begins moderately in the key of E major, in 5/4 time, or five quarter notes per measure, which can be thought of as a bar of 4/4 with an extra beat, or a bar of 3/4 plus 2/4. The verses are built primarily from the I (E), V (B), and IV (A) chords, with the vi chord (C♯m) thrown in for a little harmonic variety. Note that many of the B chords are paired with the melody note E, forming a Bsus chord (B–E–F♯). In the 12th bar of the verse, an Em chord appears from out of nowhere, hinting at the change in tonality to come several measures later.

Things shift to the key of E minor at the section marked "Rock." Featured prominently are the i (Em), vii (Dm), and VI chords (C). Starting on the syllable "peo," a ii–V progression (Am–D) is sequenced down a whole step (to G–C), setting up the last eight bars of the section. Look out for the change from 5/4 to 3/4 here, and notice the push and pull between the Bsus chords with the 4th (E) that resolves to D♯ on the B chords. Be sure to play this section with a hard-driving beat.

Everything's Coming Up Roses (page 64)

Considered by many to be the greatest American musical ever written, *Gypsy: A Musical Fable* boasts music by Jule Styne, lyrics by Stephen Sondheim, and a book by Arthur Laurents. Most often referred to simply as *Gypsy*, the musical was inspired by *Gypsy: A Memoir,* written in 1957 by the renowned burlesque entertainer Gypsy Rose Lee. The first production on Broadway opened on May 21, 1959, was nominated for seven Tony Awards, and played for 702 performances. Produced by David Merrick, directed and choreographed by Jerome Robbins, it starred Sandra Church in the title role, and featured Ethel Merman, Jack Klugman, and Maria Karnilova. Seven revivals have been staged over the years, and the musical has been adapted twice for film by Hollywood.

The lively "Everything's Coming Up Roses," the final song of Act I, finds mother Rose vowing to make her daughter Louise a big star. Following a four-bar intro, the tune, in the key of C major, kicks off with the classic chord progression ii–V–I, in this case Dm7–G7♯5–C6. The G7♯5 (G–B–D♯–F) chord includes an altered note — the raised 5th, D♯ — which creates tension that is released when the note moves down to the root (C) of the C6 chord. In other instances, the V chord appears in unaltered forms, as G7 (G–B–D–F) and G9 (G–B–D–F–A). Listen carefully for the different sounds of these similar chords.

 Another nifty thing: Note how the bass line moves down in half steps, from E to E♭, then to D (on the Dm7 chord), to start a new ii–V–I in the fifth bar after the repeat. Later, in bar 20 of the section, an E♭dim7 chord is used to approach another ii–V–I. Made from stacks of minor 3rds, a diminished 7th chord (1–3–♭5–♭7) is completely symmetrical and is often used to spice up a progression by approaching a diatonic chord (a chord occurring within the key) from a half step above or below. Take the time to get all of this song's jazzy chords under your fingers before working everything up to a bright tempo.

Gonna Build a Mountain (page 70)

The book, music, and lyrics to the 1961 musical *Stop the World — I Want to Get Off* were the work of one of Britain's strongest writing teams of the 1950s and 1960s, Leslie Bricusse and Anthony Newley. Set at a circus, the story finds the protagonist Littlechap trying to improve his life by marrying his boss's daughter, Evie, then struggling to accept the responsibilities that come with fatherhood. Littlechap deals with his problems by throwing himself into the arms of other women, only to realize many years later that what he needed all along was right in front of him — the love of Evie.

The original production of *Stop the World* opened on London's West End on July 20, 1961, and went on to run for 485 performances. Newley directed and also starred as Littlechap, while Anna Quayle played Evie as well as the other women in Littlechap's life. The Broadway production, starring Newley and Quayle, opened on October 3, 1962 and had a 555-performance run.

This brisk song is played in the key of E♭ major. In the verse, the first several measures alternate between the I (E♭) and IV chords (A♭/B♭). On the IV, the use of a non-chord-tone bass note (A♭), which could be thought of as forming a colorful V chord, B♭9sus4 (with A♭ as the ♭7, C the 9, and E♭ the 4), makes for an interesting, wide-open sounding sonority. The second part of the verse is built around a ii–V–I progression (Fm7–B♭7–E♭7). Note the use of three different I chords — E♭ (E♭–G–B♭), E♭6 (E♭–G–C), and E♭7 (E♭–G–B♭–D♭) — to create harmonic variety.

The song also makes clever use of *modulations*. Sections move up by half-step increments, musically depicting the growth of the mountain. At the third bar of the third ending, the music shifts from the key of E♭ to E, and the last eight bars are an additional half step higher, in F. Here's a valuable exercise for an aspiring accompanist: Try playing the last section a half step higher than notated, in the key of F♯/G♭ major.

Hello, Dolly! (page 74)

Featuring lyrics and music by Jerry Herman and a book by Michael Stewart, *Hello, Dolly!* tells a story whose origins can be traced back to *A Day Well Spent*, an 1835 English play by John Oxenford. This in turn inspired informed *Einen Jux will er sich machen (He Intends to Have a Fling)*, an 1842 work by the Viennese writer Johann Nestroy, which was the source of Thornton Wilder's 1938 farce *The Merchant of Yonkers*. He rewrote his play in 1955, calling it *The Matchmaker*, and this was the direct precursor to *Hello, Dolly!*

The protagonist of this irresistible musical is Mrs. Dolly Levi, who schemes to marry a "half-millionaire," Horace Vandergelder, then make good use of his money. In the end, Dolly gets her man, who is overjoyed at having been gotten. The original Broadway production, which opened on January 16, 1964, was directed and choreographed by Gower Champion and produced by David Merrick, and featured Carol Channing in the title role. The able cast included David Burns (Horace), Charles Nelson Reilly (Cornelius), and Eileen Brennan (Irene). *Hello, Dolly!* proved one of the most popular musicals of the 1960s, running for 2,844 performances. It won 10 Tony Awards in its first season, a record that stood unbroken until *The Producers* won 12 in 2001. "Hello, Dolly!" is heard in Act II. It has proven a pop hit, recorded by numerous artists, most famously by Louis Armstrong in 1964.

Arranged here in the key of B♭, the song makes extensive use of jazzy harmonies. In the first measure are two types of dominant 7th (1–3–5–♭7) chords, C13 (C–E–G–B♭–D–A) and C9♯5 (C–E–G♯–B♭–D). A 13th chord adds several notes on top of a regular 7th chord (1–3–5–♭7–9–11–13); in a typical piano voicing, the 11 is commonly omitted. A C9♯5 chord adds one note (the 9) and raises the 5th by a half step (1–3–♯5–♭7–9). Be sure to get both chords firmly under your fingers and in your mind's ear. The song also includes some major 7th chords, built by adding the 7 to a major triad (1–3–5–7). This one extra note lends a wistful quality. Seen beginning in the 13th bar is yet another neat harmonic move, heard in sophisticated jazz and pop tunes, between three C minor-type chords. Cm(maj7) is a C minor triad (C–E♭–G) with a major 7th (B), and Cm7 is C minor triad with a minor 7th (B♭). In this move, note the chromatically descending line (C–B–B♭) formed between the chords. In your own songs, try using this move to spice up a minor triad.

Hey, Look Me Over *(page 77)*

This is one of those hit tunes that lives on long after the show that generated it has been forgotten. *Wildcat,* with lyrics by Carolyn Leigh, music by Cy Coleman, and a book by N. Richard Nash, was financed by television star Lucille Ball, of *I Love Lucy* fame, and her then-husband Desi Arnaz, who invested $360,000 in exchange for 36 percent of the net profits, as well as recording and television rights. The show opened on Broadway on December 16, 1960 and drew crowds comprised largely of *I Love Lucy* fans. But lukewarm reviews, and Ball's inability to commit to the role as a result of a series of illnesses, effectively killed *Wildcat,* which ran for only 171 performances.

The protagonist of the show is Wildcat "Wildy" Jackson (Lucille Ball), who in 1912 arrives with her sister Janie in the border town of Centavo City in hopes of making a fortune in oil. She acquires a plot of land and convinces a successful foreman, Joe Dynamite (Keith Andes), to work for her. When Dynamite comes to the conclusion that Wildy is a bit of a fraud and tries to leave, she has him arrested. She subsequently arranges for his release, and the two embark on a series of misadventures. Ultimately, Dynamite confesses his love for Wildy.

"Hey, Look Me Over" is the second song in Act I. Notice that it is played in a 6/8 march — that's six eighth notes per bar. So throughout, count "*One*-two-three, *four*-five-six," emphasizing the first and fourth beats while keeping those eighth notes bouncing along.

You may find some symbols that are new to you. In the fourth bar, as well as the second bar of the second ending, is a *sforzando (sf)* mark. Meaning "forced" in Italian, this calls for the notes to be played with a strong, sudden emphasis. Throughout the piece, the cue-sized, or smaller, notes are optional — you may want to first learn the piece without them.

I Could Write a Book *(page 80)*

In the late 1930s, the American author John O'Hara, known for his keen ear for dialogue, wrote a series of short stories, presented as letters, for *The New Yorker* magazine. In 1940, the song-writer Richard Rodgers, this time in collaboration with his earlier esteemed writing partner, Lorenz Hart, turned the series into a musical, *Pal Joey.* The story, set in late-1930s Chicago, centers around an amoral, second-rate nightclub entertainer Joey Evans who dreams of owning his own nightclub. To that end he dumps his young girlfriend, Linda English, to woo an older married woman, Vera Simpson, hoping that she'll finance his project. Joey's scheme blows up in his face, and he ends up alone.

Pal Joey premiered on Broadway on December 25, 1940 and ran for 374 performances. Starring Gene Kelly as Joey and Vivienne Segal as Vera, the original production was directed by George Abbott and choreographed by Robert Alton. It enjoyed greater success, however, when it was revived in January of 1962, running for 540 performances.

Two of the songs from *Pal Joey* — "Bewitched, Bothered and Bewildered" and "I Could Write a Book" — became great American standards. In most jazz or pop interpretations of the latter tune, the first 24 bars, as shown here, are often omitted. The section features lots of ii–V–I movement (A7–D7–G) in G. Note the use of the *secondary dominant* chord, A7, which is the V of the original V chord (D7). At bar 25, we settle into the meat of the song, a 32-bar structure that sits firmly in the key of C major, starting with some I–V (C–G7) movement in the first four bars. Things get spiced up in the next four bars, with a chromatic passing chord (C♯dim7) connecting the I and ii chords (C6 and Dm7, respectively).

In the ninth bar of this section is an interesting harmonic device known as *mode mixture;* the A♭7/E♭ chord is "borrowed" from the parallel key of C minor, providing an unexpected sound while smoothly connecting the C/E and Dm7 chords. The same thing happens in the 13th measure, where the E♭7/B♭ chord is borrowed to bridge the G/B and Am7 chords, and in the 27th measure, where a Gm7 chord sets up a ii–V–I in F (Gm7–C7–F). Throughout the song, go for a moderately swinging feel.

I Dreamed a Dream *(page 84)*

Les Misérables, generally regarded as the 19th century French novelist Victor Hugo's masterpiece, tracks the lives of several French citizens over a 20-year period. In 1980 the novel was made into a *through-sung* (containing little spoken dialogue) musical by composer Claude-Michel Schönberg and librettist Alain Boublil, which became one of the most celebrated shows not only in France but throughout the world.

The most prominent characters in *Les Mis,* as it is colloquially called, are Jean Valjean, a paroled convict who, in order to become an honest man, breaks his parole; Javert, the police inspector who obsesses over finding Valjean; Fantine, a young woman who becomes a prostitute in order to support her daughter, Cosette, who is adopted by Jean Valjean; and Marius, a French student who falls in love with Cosette.

The original production of *Les Mis* opened in Paris on September 17, 1980 and ran for 107 performances. Writers Herbert Kretzmer and James Fenton reworked a translation of the original French musical into an English-language version, which opened in London on September 30, 1985. It continues to be staged in its original theater, making it the longest running musical in West End history. *Les Mis* had its Broadway debut on March 12, 1987, won eight Tony Awards that season, and continues to attract huge audiences to its home on the Great White Way.

One of the musical's biggest hits, "I Dreamed a Dream," is heard in Act I, when Fantine sings about her dashed dreams and the man who left her. Arranged here in the key of E♭ major, the song is built around a repeating four-measure progression: E♭–E♭/D–Cm–E♭/B♭–A♭–A♭/G–Fm7–B♭. Note how from the E♭ chord to the Fm7, the bass line travels stepwise down the E♭ major scale (E♭–F–G–A♭–B♭–C–D).

Also note that the E♭/D and A♭/G are technically major 7th chords in 3rd inversion (7–1–3–5). Meanwhile, the Fm7–B♭ change is a ii–V progression that sets up a return to the I chord (E♭) at the beginning of the progression. Beginning in the 20th measure, things get rather interesting harmonically. A C chord appears from out of nowhere, acting as the V of the following measure's Fm chord, suggesting the new key of F minor. The song then travels through the keys of F minor (bars 22–23) and E♭ minor (24–25; B♭ is the new V chord) before returning to E♭ major in bar 26. A lengthier key change occurs in bar 39, where the original basic progression is transposed up a whole step, from E♭ to F major for the rest of the song. After you get a handle on all of these chords and modulations, work everything up to a moderately slow tempo.

I'll Never Fall in Love Again *(page 90)*

Burt Bacharach is one of the most significant American composers of the 20th century. His songs are distinguished by unusually shifting meters, sophisticated harmony, idiosyncratic phrasing, and unexpected modulations. In 1957, Bacharach was working at New York City's Brill Building, the Mecca of music publishing and songwriting, when he met the lyricist Hal David. They became a songwriting team and, that same year, scored a #1 hit with "The Story of My Life," recorded by Marty Robbins for Columbia Records. Four years later they began working seriously with Dionne Warwick, a conservatory-trained singer they originally used to record demos of their songs. They soon began writing tunes with her specifically in mind, resulting in one of the most successful pop collaborations ever. From the early 1960s through the early '80s, Warwick made charting hits of 38 Bacharach-penned singles. At the same time, major artists like the Beatles ("Baby, It's You"), Isaac Hayes ("Walk On By"), and Dusty Springfield ("The Look of Love") also contributed to Bacharach's success with their enduring interpretations of his songs.

"I'll Never Fall in Love Again" was a big hit from the 1968 musical *Promises, Promises.* Written by Bacharach and David, with a book by Neil Simon, the show ran on Broadway for 1,282 performances. The song became a hit for Dionne Warwick in 1970. Played here in E♭ major, it kicks off with a nice four-bar groove that alternates between the I (E♭) and Imaj7 (E♭maj7) chords. Look out here for the syncopation; in the last half of each measure, a chord appears on the "and" of the beat.

The first four bars of the verse are fairly straightforward, built on a I–vi–IV (E♭–Cm7–A♭maj7) progression. In bars 9-11, things get a little more complicated — the ii chord (Fm7) acts as a temporary i chord in a ii–V–i progression (Gm7–C7–Fm7). Then, in bar 12, the Fm7 chord acts as the ii chord of another basic ii–V–I; interestingly, the I chord (E♭) is unexpectedly delayed by an appearance of the IV7 chord (A♭7), which adds a little funkiness to the proceedings. The verse wraps up with a two-bar restatement of the intro vamp.

Throughout, a nicely rhythmic texture is formed as the bass notes fall on beats 1 and 3 and the chords on 2 and 4. To achieve the appropriate groove, be particularly mindful of rests; don't let any bass note or chord sound beyond its designated beat.

If I Loved You (page 100)

Carousel was the second of many hit musicals by Rodgers and Hammerstein. (1943's *Oklahoma!* was the first.) By this time, the pair had already transformed the musical from what had been a loose collection of songs and dances into a cohesive work of art, in this case built around a tragic story line. This in itself was highly unusual in musical theater, a medium designed to leave its audiences smiling.

Carousel, based on a 1909 play by Ferenc Molnar called *Liliom*, is set in a New England village and tells the sad story of a mill girl, Julie Jordan, who marries a handsome but coarse carousel barker, Billy Bigelow. Their union is anything but harmonious and things quickly turn very sour for the couple. After Julie becomes pregnant, Billy and a friend make plans to rob the mill owner, David Bascombe, but the attempt is foiled and Billy commits suicide. When he is allowed to return to Earth fifteen years later, he remains a great failure, because he is unable to show his love for his wife and daughter.

The original Broadway production, starring Jan Clayton as Julie and John Raitt as Billy, was directed by Rouben Mamoulian, opened on April 19, 1945, and ran for 890 performances. A two-year national tour followed, and the musical has since enjoyed a handful of revivals.

"If I Loved You" is heard Acts I and II, when Julie and Billy attempt to express their love for each other. The song kicks off in the key of D major in 2/4 time. As directed by the tempo marking *allegretto moderato,* play the piece moderately fast and cheerful.

Here's something neat — the accompaniment of the first eight bars of the verse, played on one big D chord, are essentially the same as the next eight bars, which are moved down to D♭, a chord that incidentally is foreign to the key. So after you learn the first eight bars, just lower everything (except for the melody) down a half step, and the next eight bars should fall into place — an excellent exercise in the invaluable skill of transposing.

In the 17th bar of the verse, we return to D major via its V chord, A major. Notice how smoothly this happens with the same melody note — the pitch D♭ (root of the D♭ chord) is the same as C♯ (3rd of the A chord). Several bars later, there's both a change of meter, to 4/4, and of key, to C major, so really make sure to transition smoothly in that spot.

In the refrain, during which you'll slow things down, the music gets a bit more complicated, with several layers going on at once, so work this section up one measure at a time, making sure that everything sounds even and flowing.

It's a Grand Night for Singing (page 104)

In 1945, Rodgers and Hammerstein scored five songs for the movie musical *State Fair,* which was a Technicolor remake of the 1933 movie of the same name, directed by Henry King. The movie was remade again, in 1962, with Rodgers composing new materials; unfortunately, it failed to meet critical and financial success. Then, in 1995, *State Fair* was adapted into a Broadway musical, with additional songs, such as "When I Go Out Walking with My Baby" (*Oklahoma!*), borrowed from several other Rodgers and Hammerstein musicals to flesh things out. In the stage production, the plot of which is similar to that of the previous incarnations, the farming family Frake take a three-day trip to the Iowa State Fair during the mid '40s. The parents, Abel and Melissa, hope to win blue ribbons for their boar and mincemeat, while the siblings, Margy and Wayne, cruise the midway and find romance.

The musical opened, fittingly, on August 12, 1995, at the Iowa State Fair. Starting on March 27, 1996, it ran on Broadway for 110 performances. The cast of the latter production included John Davidson (Abel), Kathryn Crosby (Melissa), Andrea McArdle (Margy), and Ben Wright (Wayne).

"It's a Grand Night for Singing" was featured in the original film and is sung by the company to close out Act I of the musical. The song is a waltz, so play it at a danceable tempo, emphasizing the first beat of each bar. To further ensure that you achieve the proper rhythmic feel, pay careful attention to the duration of each note in the piece. For instance, in the bass clef of bar 8 are the notes G and D. While it may be tempting to play both notes together for the full measure, note that only the D, which is a dotted-half note, is sustained. So be sure to lift your finger from the quarter-note G right after beat 1, to prevent it from ringing through. Also, throughout the piece be mindful of the *slurs* — curved lines connecting a series of notes, indicating that they are to be played *legato,* or without separation.

In the eighth bar of the piece is a symbol you may not have previously encountered — *gliss.,* short for *glissando* — a glide from one pitch to another. At that spot, simply slide your fingers upwards across the white keys, from the D beside middle C to the D an octave higher, arriving at that note squarely on beat 1 of bar 9. If you execute the technique properly, you should be able to clearly hear the pitches of the in-between white keys. Also, look out for the downward *glissandi,* from E to G or F, occurring later in the piece.

The Lady Is a Tramp (page 108)

With music by Richard Rodgers and lyrics by Lorenz Hart, *Babes in Arms* is a musical set around the story of a group of youths whose parents are out-of-work performers. They put on a show to avoid being sent to work on a farm. Their show is a flop, but through a serendipitous incident, the players are subsequently able to put on a successful production and make their own youth center. In any case, *Babes* was bold in that it made a satire of racism. The youngsters' production, for instance, is financed under the condition that two African-Americans not perform in the show. The bankroller, of course, is later rebuked.

Directed by Robert Sinclair and choreographed by George Balanchine, *Babes* opened on Broadway on April 14, 1937 and ran for 289 performances. Although it received rave reviews on opening night, ticket agencies did little to help out the musical (in fact, slashing ticket prices), perhaps because of its comparatively clean and wholesome nature. But by July 17th of that year, every competing show on Broadway had folded, allowing *Babes* to really take off, and in 1939 it was made into a film version starring Mickey Rooney and Judy Garland.

The musical featured several tunes that became popular standards, including "My Funny Valentine," "Where or When," and "The Lady Is a Tramp." The latter song is a spoof of uppity New York society, with all its rules and codes. It has been covered by numerous artists, most notably Frank Sinatra, Ella Fitzgerald, and Shirley Bassey, each of whom used it as a signature song, and it was also sung by Lena Horne for the film *Words and Music,* a fictionalized biography of Rodgers and Hart. A great way to get well acquainted with a standard is to listen to a number of different interpretations, so try and check out these and other versions before delving into the arrangement.

When you're ready to learn the song, arranged here in the key of C major, be sure to play it moderately and "properly," befitting, say, of a society dinner. In other words, sort of tongue-in-cheek. And while the music is fairly straightforward, be aware of all the accidentals. In each Cm7 bar (which is borrowed from the parallel key, C minor), for instance, be ready to grab the notes B♭ and E♭.

Let's Hang On (page 95)

A *jukebox musical* is one that is built from previously composed songs, often by a single group or artist. Some, such as *Lennon* (2005), about the life of John Lennon and with music from his solo years, have failed to achieve success, causing writers to avoid the jukebox musical altogether, but the relatively recent *Jersey Boys* has helped popularize the style. With a book by Marshall Brickman, music by Bob Gaudio and lyrics by Bob Crewe, *Jersey Boys* tells the story of Frankie Valli and the Four Seasons — Frankie Valli, Bob Gaudio, Tommy DeVito, and Nick Massi — from their blue-collar roots to their astounding success as an Italian-American pop-rock group. The show includes their biggest hits, "Sherry," "Big Girls Don't Cry," and "Oh, What a Night," among others.

Directed by Des McAnuff and starring Christian Hoff (Tommy DeVito), Daniel Reichard (Bob Gaudio), J. Robert Spencer (Nick Massi), and John Lloyd Young (Frankie Valli), the musical opened on Broadway on November 6, 2005 and was an instant smash. The show won four Tony Awards, including Best Musical. The first national *Jersey Boys* tour began in San Francisco on December 10, 2006, and a production opened in London on March 18, 2008.

Heard in the second act, "Let's Hang On" was a hit for the Four Seasons in 1965, reaching #3 position on the *Billboard* Hot 100 singles chart. (It also became a hit for Barry Manilow, in 1982.) The song featured a number of interesting devices, including an infectious arrangement incorporating two fuzz guitars, as well as the group's trademark hook-laden falsetto vocals. Cleverly, one guitar part is incorporated into the piano arrangement beginning in the sixth measure. Note that to emulate the guitar's range, this part is played on the piano with the right hand in the bass clef. Also notice how chromatic *passing tones* — foreign notes that connect notes within a key, like the D♯ between the D and the E — add plenty of sass.

In bar 8, the left hand joins in on the fun with an approximation of the part originally played on electric bass. So, in that spot, and for the rest of the song, try to think like a bassist and make all of those single notes really solid and grooving. Meanwhile, the remaining right-hand work is taken from the original vocal melody and harmonies; if needed, learn that part on its own before adding the electrifying bass line.

Mama, I'm a Big Girl Now (page 146)

The 1988 film *Hairspray* was quite a departure for director John Waters, who was known for his dark cult films. But while fairly mainstream and campy, *Hairspray* managed to examine tough racial issues through the lens of Waters' characteristically idiosyncratic sense of humor. In 2002, the film was made into a musical, with music by Marc Shaiman, lyrics by Scott Wittman and Shaiman, and a book by Mark O'Donnell and Thomas Meehan. Set in 1962 Baltimore, *Hairspray* finds Tracy Turnblad, a corpulent teen-aged girl with a passion for dancing, winning a spot on a television dance program. She then sets out to defeat the show's reigning champion and win the heart of the hunky Link Larkin, while racially integrating the show.

Produced by Jack O'Brien and choreographed by Jerry Mitchell, *Hairspray* hit Broadway on August 15, 2002 and is still running there. The original cast included Marissa Jaret Winokur (Tracy Turnblad) and Harvey Fierstein (Tracy's mother, Edna Turnblad). The musical has seen productions in a number of other cities, from Toronto to Tokyo, and won 8 Tony Awards out of 13 nominations. In 2007, *Hairspray* made its way back onto film as a musical starring Nikki Blonsky as Tracy Turnblad and John Travolta as Edna Turnblad.

The score of *Hairspray* is rife with 1960s dance and blues numbers. Especially fun is the rebellious "Mama, I'm a Big Girl Now," a song in the key of F major, with a verse built from the time-honored I–vi–IV–V (F–Dm–B♭–C) progression. You'll want to play the eight-bar intro freely, as directed, accenting each new chord as indicated by the *sforzando* marking.

In the ninth bar you can see the indication for a *shuffle* — a common and infectious R&B rhythm in which the beat is divided into two unequal parts but normally notated conventionally. You could count the shuffle feel as "One-uh-let, two-uh-let, three-uh-let, four-uh-let," and so on, with the second eighth note of a beat falling on the "let." Or, when playing a succession of swung eighth notes, just think long-short, long-short, and so on.

Heads-up — don't be surprised by the six flats at the beginning of bar 51—everything is simply moved up by a half step, to the key of G♭ major, for a dramatic effect. The same thing happens in bar 85, where things shift up an additional half step, to the easier-to-play key of G. Be sure to make each modulation even more exciting by faithfully observing the change in dynamics.

Mamma Mia (page 156)

While the jukebox musical *Jersey Boys* was based on the real-life experiences of a musical group, *Mamma Mia!* has a fictional plot, written by the British playwright Catherine Johnson and incorporating the songs of the Swedish pop group ABBA, which were composed by Benny Andersson and Björn Ulvaeus. The story is set on a dreamy Greek island and centers around a single mother, Donna Sheridan, coping with the marriage of her young daughter, Sophie. Sophie attempts to learn the identity of her father, while three men from her mother's past return for the first time in two decades.

Mamma Mia! opened in London on April 6, 1999, with a cast including Siobhán McCarthy (Donna), Louise Plowright (Tanya), and Jenny Galloway (Rosie). The original Broadway production opened on October 18, 2001, with a cast including Louise Pitre (Donna), Karen Mason (Tanya), and Judy Kaye (Rosie). It is now one of the longest-running Broadway musicals of all time and has been made into a film starring Pierce Brosnan and Meryl Streep.

Mamma Mia! includes such ABBA hits as "Dancing Queen," "Mamma Mia," and "Voulez Vous." "Mamma Mia" was from the group's third album, *ABBA*, and in 1975 topped the Australian charts for 11 weeks. The song is heard in Act I of the musical, as well as in the encore, during which audience participation is encouraged. "Mamma Mia" has a driving rock beat, so throughout add a little emphasis to each beat 1 and 3, even though no accents are indicated in the music. Everything should be fairly easy to play — the simple, single-note bass line allows you to concentrate on those right-hand block chords.

"Mamma Mia" is mostly *diatonic,* which means that the notes fall within the key, but in the intro and after the second ending, you'll notice a number of A♯ notes. This accidental belongs to a D+, or D augmented chord. An *augmented triad* is like a major triad (1–3–5), only with the 5th raised by a half step (1–3–♯5), creating a rather tense sound. Listen for the dramatic push and pull between the A♯ and A.

Memory *(page 139)*

Written by Andrew Lloyd Webber, *Cats* is a musical based on T.S. Eliot's *Old Possum's Book of Practical Cats,* a children's book with witty poems about assorted felines. The poems, which Webber first heard as a child, are the lyrics for his musical, in which cats are called "Jellicles." *Cats* is set in a junkyard on the night of the annual Jellicle Ball, where the cats get together to dance under the full moon. The plot involves the cats, played by actors in unitards, tails, and wigs, introducing each other to the audience. At the end of the ball, Old Deuteronomy, the leader of the Jellicles, takes a selected cat, Grizabella, to Heaviside Layer, or cat heaven.

Originally produced by Cameron Mackintosh, directed by Trevor Nunn, and choreographed by Gillian Lynne, *Cats* debuted in London's West End on May 11, 1981. It ran for a total of 8,949 performances (surpassed only by *Les Misérables,* in 1986), ending on May 11, 2002, when it was broadcasted on a large screen in Covent Garden, for those unable to secure tickets.

Cats made its New York debut on October 7, 1982 with the same production team and on June 19, 1997 became the longest-running musical in Broadway history, with 6,138 performances. *Cats* went on for a total of 7,485 performances, closing on Broadway on September 10, 2000. It was surpassed as longest-running musical by Webber's *The Phantom of the Opera,* in 2006.

Sung by Grizabella, "Memory" is the most famous song from *Cats*. It is in the *compound meter* (each measure is divided into three or more parts) of 12/8 — that's twelve eighth notes per bar — a time signature common not only in classical music but also in blues and doo wop. When playing the music, it's helpful to count "*One*-two-three, *four*-five-six, *seven*-eight-nine, *ten*-eleven-twelve," and so on, adding a little emphasis squarely on each beat while making sure that the eighth notes flow smoothly together. To help get the feel of 12/8 down, listen to a recording of "Memory," then learn the first six bars and play them repeatedly.

After you get a handle on 12/8, notice that at several points in the piece, the meter changes, so for the 10/8 and 6/8 measures, be prepared to drop, respectively, two and six beats. At first, take things slowly so that you can transition between these changing time signatures without speeding up or slowing down.

My Romance *(page 162)*

With the effects of the Great Depression still reverberating, the mid-1930s were a tough time for America, but a fruitful time for the team of Rodgers and Hart, who, starting with *Jumbo* (1935) enjoyed a string of musical hits until Hart's death in 1943. *Jumbo* was about a war between competing circuses, the only show on Broadway ever to feature live animals. In fact, at the climax of the show, the lead player, Jimmy Durante, who starred as Claudius B. Bowers, went as far as to lie down and accept a live elephant's foot upon his head. The original production, which opened on Broadway on November 16, 1935 and ran for 233 performances, also starred Gloria Grafton (Mickey Considine) and Donald Novis (Matt Mulligan, Jr.). In 1962, the musical was rewritten as a film titled *Billy Rose's Jumbo,* starring Durante, along with Doris Day, Martha Raye, and Stephen Boyd.

The most popular songs from *Jumbo* are "Little Girl Blue," "The Most Beautiful Girl in the World," and "My Romance." The latter is heard when the romantic leads fall in love while feeding the circus animals, and has been recorded by everyone from Frank Sinatra to Lou Rawls. And, in fact, the two halves of the epitome of rock-pop marriage — James Taylor and Carly Simon — have each recorded their own versions in the years since their divorce. As with many Broadway tunes that have become pop and jazz favorites, a standard interpretation normally omits the verse, and starts with the refrain.

While the song is arranged here in the "easy" key of C major, the accompaniment might be a bit tricky in some spots. So, when learning the piece, play just the melody (in the right hand, the upstemmed notes or highest note of chord) and bass parts. Later, when you combine everything, make sure that the melody really stands out and sings. For instance, in the second measure of the refrain, without being too forceful — remember, "My Romance" is a smooth and expressive song — add emphasis to the highest note of each chord. In the third bar of the refrain, make sure that the melody note C, played on beat 1 and ringing through beat 4, doesn't become obscured by the decorative melody of G, G♭, and F. Also, for the appropriate phrasing, be sure to carefully follow the slur indications throughout.

Ol' Man River (page 166)

Jerome Kern was one of America's finest composers of popular music, with over 700 songs to his name, including "Smoke Gets in Your Eyes" and "The Way You Look Tonight." In the mid-1920s, Kern met Oscar Hammerstein II, who would become a close friend and collaborator. Their 1927 musical *Show Boat* is considered one of the first American musicals. It differed from the typical revues of the era in that it was based on a dramatic plot containing themes of racism and mixed blood. It was also the first racially integrated show, in which black and white actors performed together. It paved the way for others to write musicals with more mature themes. Still, it has been both praised for promoting racial tolerance and condemned for its caricatures of African-Americans.

Show Boat was based on the book of the same name by Edna Ferber. The story begins in the 1880s on a riverboat, the *Cotton Blossom,* and centers around a troupe working under Cap'n Andy and his wife, Parthy Ann. Decades later, the players reunite en route to Hollywood, and woven throughout the musical, the story of the African-American couple of Joe and Queenie reveals the harshness of racism.

Produced by Florenz Ziegfeld and choreographed by Sammy Lee, *Show Boat* opened on Broadway on December 27, 1927 and ran for 575 performances. It opened in London on May 3, 1928 and ran for 350 performances. As issues associated with race persisted through the decades, the musical went on to enjoy several film versions as well as several revivals, the latest of which was in 1994 and which earned a Tony Award for Best Revival.

One of *Show Boat's* best-known songs, "Ol' Man River," was originally written for the bass singer and actor Paul Robeson, whose recording of the tune for the 1936 version of the film is the most famous rendition. Written from the point of view of a dockworker, the song speaks of African-American struggles and is tied into the flow of the Mississippi River.

"Ol' Man River" is in the somewhat challenging key of E♭ major, with plenty of accidentals throughout. So in learning the song, be sure to take things slowly and scan ahead for flats, sharps, and cancellations. Also, to achieve the proper flow, be mindful of the rhythmic layers. For example, make sure you hold the notes B and G throughout bars 2 and 3 while adding the surrounding chords. And throughout, where you see a squiggly vertical line, quickly roll the chord, from lowest note to highest, to add emotional heft.

On a Clear Day (You Can See Forever) (page 176)

On a Clear Day You Can See Forever was the successful 1965 collaboration by lyricist Alan Jay Lerner and composer Burton Lane. Alan Jay Lerner, of course, was best known for his long-running partnership with composer Frederick Loewe, a teaming that created such Broadway mega-hits as *Brigadoon, My Fair Lady, Paint Your Wagon,* and *Camelot.* Burton Lane, a protégé of George Gershwin, deserved more fame and respect during his lifetime. A prodigious and witty composer, Lane wrote extensively for both Broadway and Hollywood, making his biggest splash with *Finian's Rainbow* (with lyricist E.Y. "Yip" Harburg) in 1947 and *On a Clear Day.* He was also the man who discovered a very young Judy Garland, bringing her to the attention of MGM.

One of the great musicals set in Manhattan, *On a Clear Day* is about a kooky young lady with low self-esteem named Daisy Gamble who visits a hypnotist to help her stop smoking. During the treatment, Daisy's trances reveal her extraordinary "past lives" throughout history. The musical opened on Broadway on October 17, 1965 and played for 280 performances. Barbara Harris originated the role of Daisy. Barbra Streisand portrayed Daisy in a 1970 movie version.

The title song is one of those golden-age, inspirational showstoppers like "Climb Every Mountain" from *The Sound of Music*, but swinging enough to interest such jazz-piano greats as Oscar Peterson and Bill Evans, both of whom covered the song. Notice an abundance of accidentals — there are lots of nice, jazzy chords — so be sure to take things slowly when first learning the song, scanning ahead for upcoming chromatic notes. And be sure to isolate any areas that trip you up, playing them repetitively until they flow smoothly under your fingers.

The song has some slightly square rhythms, so unless you want to sound stiff, carefully follow all the dynamic and expressive markings. In the third bar of the intro, for example, slow down a little *(poco rit.)* and get quieter *(mp)* before returning to the original tempo *(a tempo)* at the start of the verse. As the song builds, in the 16th bar of the verse (on the syllables "You" and "feel"), increase the volume and play more expressively *(più espr.)*. Also, throughout the song, be especially mindful of the rests, silencing the bass and accompaniment notes as indicated, to sound neat and rhythmic.

On the Street Where You Live *(page 171)*

Featuring a book and lyrics by Alan Jay Lerner and music by Frederick Loewe, *My Fair Lady* is one of the most successful musicals of all time. It was adapted from *Pygmalion,* the George Bernard Shaw play of 1913. In the story, a hubristic professor of phonetics, Henry Higgins, transforms a poor Cockney girl, Eliza Doolittle, into a society lady by correcting her speech. The professor and his protégé grow close, but in the end she ostensibly rejects him.

Directed by Moss Hart and starring Rex Harrison and Julie Andrews as Higgins and Doolittle, *My Fair Lady* debuted on Broadway on March 15, 1956 and ran for 2,717 performances, then opened on London's West End on April 30, 1958, where it ran for 2,281 performances. The musical was an instant hit, and it won Tony Awards for Best Musical, Actor, and Director. Similarly, a 1964 motion picture version, starring Rex Harrison and Audrey Hepburn, won several Academy Awards. Then, from 1976 to 2001, a handful of revivals ensued, followed in 2007 by a U.S. tour.

My Fair Lady included a number of songs that became pop standards, including "I Could Have Danced All Night," "The Rain in Spain," and "On the Street Where You Live." The last song is heard in Act I and is sung by the character of Freddy Eynsford-Hill, a young man who is besotted with Doolittle. A 1956 version recorded by Vic Damone went all the way to #4 on the *Billboard* charts, and the song has been covered by many other performers, including the vocalists Nat King Cole, Harry Connick, Jr., and Bobby Darin.

"On the Street Where You Live," written here in the key of B♭ major, has a particularly expressive melody, with a number of dramatic leaps — for example, up a perfect fifth, from D to A, on the syllables "pave" and "ment," and up a major seventh, from E♭ to D, on the syllables "once" and "am."

Play each and every *crescendo* (remember, gradually get louder) and *decrescendo* (gradually get quieter), indicated by the "hairpin" marks throughout. Doing so helps ensure an emotive performance that will move an audience.

Popular *(page 180)*

Stephen Schwartz is a great American lyricist and composer best known for his hit musicals, most notably *Godspell* (1971) and *Pippin* (1972). In 1995, Schwartz encountered the Gregory Maguire novel *Wicked: The Life and Times of the Wicked Witch of the West,* which retells L. Frank Baum's *The Wonderful Wizard of Oz* from the witch's perspective. After convincing Maguire to release the rights for a stage version, Schwartz paired up with the librettist Winnie Holzman to develop a script. The result of their labor, the musical *Wicked*, begins before Dorothy arrives in Kansas and tells the story of two young witches — the ambitious, beautiful Glinda and the troubled, green-skinned Elphaba — who go on to become the Good Witch of the North and the Wicked Witch of the West.

Directed by Joe Mantello and staged by Wayne Cilento, *Wicked* opened on Broadway on October 30, 2003. It starred Kristin Chenoweth (Glinda), Idina Menzel (Elphaba), and Joel Grey (The Wizard). Although the production received some negative early reviews, it became a commercial success, spawning productions worldwide, breaking box-office records, and winning two Tony Awards in the process.

Sung by Glinda to Elphaba in Act I, "Popular" is one of the most, well, popular tunes from *Wicked*. The song has a number of different rhythmic feels. The first 17 bars, in the key of A minor, should be played very sweetly and freely. As indicated by each *colla voce* marking, the singer should set the rhythm, and the pianist should follow. It may take a bit of practice to coordinate this feel. In bar 10 are some Xs in the vocal notation. These simply mean that the pitches aren't predetermined, so for dramatic effect, try speaking, rather than singing, the syllables "I" and "know." Finally, the *ten.* at the end of the section means *tenuto* — hold the notes just slightly longer than normal.

The next section, marked "Bright and bubbly," moves to the key of F major and has a swing feel — whenever there's a pair of eighth notes, remember to play or sing the first note for longer than the second, unless otherwise directed by the bracketed indication *straight 8ths*. Throughout, strive for a playfully rhythmic feel, being mindful of the many left-hand rests.

Put On a Happy Face *(page 189)*

Bye Bye Birdie has a book by Michael Stewart, lyrics by Lee Adams, and music by Charles Strouse. In the story, an Elvis Presley–like superstar, Conrad Birdie, is drafted into the army. His agent's secretary, Rosie Alvarez, comes up with a final publicity stunt — on *The Ed Sullivan Show,* Conrad will sing "One Last Kiss" and do just that to one of his adoring female fans. Naturally, complications arise.

Produced by Edward Padula and directed and choreographed by Gower Champion, *Bye Bye Birdie* opened on Broadway on April 14, 1960 and ran for 607 performances, winning Tony Awards for Best Musical, Director, Choreography, and Supporting or Featured Actor. Included in the original cast were Dick Van Dyke (Conrad's agent, Albert Peterson), Chita Rivera (Rosie), and Dick Gautier (Conrad). The show opened in London on June 15, 1961, running for 268 performances. Van Dyke also starred in a 1963 film version, and a 1995 television version featured Jason Alexander, of *Seinfeld* fame, as Albert Peterson.

Heard in Act I, "Put On a Happy Face" has become a pop and jazz standard, interpreted by everyone from guitarist Tal Farlow to vocalist and pianist Blossom Dearie. Played here in the key of E♭ major, the song is built from a handful of jazz chords, many of which are *close-voiced,* which means that some of the notes of the chord are moved up or down an octave so that several notes are clustered close to one another. Take, for instance, the B♭9 chord in bar 7, in which the top two notes, D (the third) and C (ninth), are a major second apart, and the lowest note, A♭ (seventh) is a major third below the C. Voicing a chord in this manner makes for a rather sophisticated sound. Play the B♭9 voicing as shown in the music, then play just a standard root-position B♭9 chord, lowest note to highest, B♭–D–F–A♭–C. Hear the difference?

In reading the notation, don't be confused when the same note is played in two different layers. In bar 5, for example, you obviously wouldn't play two B♭s on beat 1, for the piano only has one B♭ key. What's happening here is that on beat 1, the B♭ functions as a melody note, but becomes an accompaniment note as it is held through beat 2. Also, throughout, be sure to give the melody notes (upstemmed) a little extra emphasis, to make them stand apart from the accompaniment, which is in close proximity.

Real Live Girl (page 192)

The American playwright and screenplay writer Neil Simon is one of Broadway's most celebrated writers, with such hit works as *Barefoot in the Park* (1963), *Sweet Charity* (1966), and *Brighton Beach Memoirs* (1983). *Little Me* was written by Simon, with music by Cy Coleman and lyrics by Carolyn Leigh. The show is based on the Patrick Dennis book *Little Me, The Intimate Memoirs of That Great Star of Stage, Screen and Television, Belle Poitrine* (1961), a farcical, risqué autobiography of an imaginary diva, replete with photographs. The musical tells the story of a poor girl named Belle Poitrine, who gathers fame and fortune with the assistance of a series of sympathetic gentlemen.

Directed by Cy Feuer and Bob Fosse and with Tony-winning choreography from Fosse, *Little Me* debuted on Broadway on November 17, 1962 and ran for 257 performances. The show starred Sid Caesar in multiple roles, along with Virginia Martin (Young Belle) and Nancy Andrews (Old Belle). Meanwhile, the London production, featuring Bruce Forsyth and Eileen Gorlay, opened on November 18, 1964 and ran for 334 performances, and the musical enjoyed several revivals, in 1982, 1984, and 1998.

"Real Live Girl" is the most popular song from *Little Me*. Based in the key of G major, this little waltz has got a bit of syncopation, especially in the first eight bars, so it's important to play very close attention to the rhythms — remember, a waltz is for dancing. At first, it may be helpful to count "One-and, two-and, three-and" throughout, so that you can feel exactly where the notes should fall. For example, in the treble clef of measures 5–8, each of the downstemmed notes falls on an "and."

In addition to infectious rhythms, "Real Live Girl" has got plenty of interesting chords. Take for example, G7♯5 and F7♯11. Dominant seventh chords with these types of alterations (the ♯5 and ♯11) are among the defining sounds of jazz harmony. The ♯5 of G7 is D♯, and the ♯11 of F7 is B; try playing each chord without its alteration, to hear the dramatic difference just one note can make in a chord. And for fun, in other songs with 7th chords, experiment with determining and adding ♯5s and ♯11s.

Satin Doll (page 195)

Edward Kennedy "Duke" Ellington was one of the most significant composers not just of jazz but of American music in general. As a bandleader, Ellington wrote with the specific capabilities of each of his musicians in mind. Many of his band members were jazz giants in their own right, and the music that Ellington wrote often transcended category. While Ellington delighted in using extended forms more akin to classical music, such as those of *Black, Brown, and Beige* (1943) and *The Far East Suite* (1966), he is most widely known for brilliant, conventionally structured songs, including "Mood Indigo" (1930), "It Don't Mean a Thing (If It Ain't Got That Swing)" (1932), "Sophisticated Lady" (1933), and so many others.

These three tunes are among those included in *Sophisticated Ladies,* a musical based on the songs of Ellington, with a concept by Donald McKayle, musical and dance arrangements by Lloyd Mayers, and vocal arrangements by Malcolm Dodds and Lloyd Mayers. The revue opened on Broadway on March 1, 1981 and ran for 767 performances with a cast including Ellington's son, Mercer; Gregory Hines; Phyllis Hyman; and Judith Jamison.

Composed in 1953, the Ellington song "Satin Doll" had lyrics added later by Johnny Mercer (one of America's greatest songwriters in his own right and a cofounder of Capitol Records) and Billy Strayhorn (Ellington's closest collaborator). In this incarnation, the song became an enduring standard, with notable recorded interpretations by Ella Fitzgerald and Frank Sinatra.

While it was composed in the "easy" key of C major, "Satin Doll" frequently travels outside of that key, starting with the chromatic passing chords (E♭m7, D♭m7, and C♯m7) in the four-bar introduction. Although the music, replete with complex chords and extensive accidentals, may seem complicated, the tune is based on the standard 32-bar AABA form. So, in learning the first A section (bars 5–12), you'll essentially be learning three-quarters of the song.

There's a certain type of repetition within each section, too. Compare the A section's first two bars (bars 5–6 of the song) and second two bars, and you'll find that the music is essentially identical but transposed up a whole step, from the ii–V progression Dm7–G7 to Em7–A7. A similar thing happens between the first four measures and second four measures of the bridge (bars 21–28 of the song) — a phrase that revolves around the progression Gm7–C7 is transposed up a step, centering around Am7–D7. Most important, having a handle of a song's architecture can greatly enhance the learning process.

Seasons of Love (page 198)

Jonathan Larson was a New York City playwright and composer who dealt with heavy issues like the AIDS epidemic and chemical addiction. His most important work was the rock opera *Rent,* which was the among the first musicals to feature gay and transgender characters and was intended to speak to a younger, more liberal generation of theatergoers. Basically a retelling of the Giacomo Puccini opera *La Bohème, Rent* was set in late-1980s Alphabet City — then a seedy-but-creative section of New York's East Village — instead of Paris and featured young artists struggling to live and work in the shadow of AIDS, as opposed to tuberculosis.

Larson died tragically on January 25, 1996, never seeing his show produced on Broadway. *Rent* opened on April 29, 1996. It closed on June 1, 2008, making it one of the longest-running musicals of all time, to say nothing of a cultural phenomenon. In 1996, it was nominated for ten Tony Awards and won four, including Best Musical. That same year, it also won the Pulitzer Prize for Drama. In 2005, the musical was adapted into a motion picture starring many of the original cast members, with selected songs changed to dialogue, to better suit the medium.

"Seasons of Love" is one of the most popular numbers from *Rent.* The song, which addresses the passage of time, is sung by the entire cast at the beginning of the second act. On the original soundtrack is an alternate version with R&B great Stevie Wonder, and pop legend Donny Osmond has also covered "Seasons." Interestingly, the powerful song has a very simple structure: The first four bars, played in the key of F major, introduce an *ostinato,* or repeated figure, over which most of the lyrics are sung. So, in learning the song, make sure that you have the ostinato down cold before proceeding to the verse, and everything should fall smoothly into place. In the even bars, be sure to crisply articulate the dotted-eighth–16th–eighth-rest–eighth rhythm, which is crucial to the song's rock feel.

In bar 21, while the music may appear completely different, the four-bar ostinato is basically just transposed up a fourth, to center around a B♭ chord, adjusted rhythmically, and played twice. So, if you learned the first section properly, this one should be a breeze and you'll now have the whole song down.

She Loves Me (page 208)

The musical *She Loves Me* has a book by Joe Masteroff, with lyrics and music by, respectively, Sheldon Harnick and Jerry Bock — the same team responsible for *Fiddler on the Roof* (1964). *She Loves Me* is an adaptation of the Hungarian playwright Miklos Laszlo's *Parfumerie,* which also inspired the 1940 film *The Shop around the Corner,* the 1949 musical *In the Good Old Summertime,* and the 1998 movie *You've Got Mail.*

Set in 1930s Budapest, the musical tells the story of two salespeople, Georg Nowack and Amalia Balash, who have a difficult relationship at work and who, unbeknownst to each other, are secret romantic pen pals. Directed by Harold Prince and choreographed by Carol Haney, *She Loves Me* had its Broadway debut on April 23, 1963 and ran for 302 performances. The original cast included Daniel Massey as Georg and Barbara Cook as Amalia. It opened on London's West End on April 29, 1964, featuring Gary Raymond and Anne Rogers and running for 189 performances. The show was nominated for five Tony Awards and won one, and had Broadway and West End revivals in 1993 and 1994, respectively.

One of the most popular numbers in *She Loves Me,* the title song is sung in Act II by Georg. Played in the key of F major, the song kicks off with a *quintuplet* — in this case, five 16th notes in the space normally occupied by four. To learn the rhythm, start with just a single note, repeating it five times on each beat, counting "One-quin-tup-uh-let, two-quin-tup-uh-let, three-quin-tup-uh-let, four-quin-tup-uh-let," etc. As for the *rubato* indication, for the first full nine bars, feel free to speed up or slow down according to your own discretion.

The arrangement is one that gets the most out of very streamlined musical materials. The verse starts off very simply, with just the melody and a bass line and adds block chords here and there to add interest as the song progresses. In bar 35, the bass line is doubled at the octave. In conjunction with block chords, this textural change generates even further interest.

Somebody Loves Me (page 212)

A *revue* is an irreverent multi-act theater show combining music, dance, and drama sketches. This format was most popular in America from the mid-1910s to the early 1930s. Some of the most notable Broadway examples were the *Ziegfeld Follies,* mounted by the impresario Florenz Ziegfeld from 1907–1931. These in turn inspired *George White's Scandals,* which ran from 1911–1939, and which helped propel the careers of such stars as W.C. Fields, Ethel Merman, and the Three Stooges. *The Scandals* from 1920–1924 featured early work of the composer George Gershwin, who came to combine orchestral, Yiddish, and blues sounds, among others, into a distinctly American song style that crossed over from Broadway to classical audiences.

With music by Gershwin and lyrics by B.G. DeSylva and Ballard MacDonald, "Somebody Loves Me" first appeared in *George White's Scandals of 1924,* where it was sung by Winnie Lightner. The number has been covered extensively by everyone from jazz luminaries like Duke Ellington to pop vocalists like Julie London to guitar legends like Les Paul. One of the most successful, though not as musically rewarding, versions was recorded in 1952 by the Four Lads, a Canadian pop vocal group. It went all the way to #22 on the *Billboard* charts.

Arranged here in the key of G major, "Somebody Loves Me" has the same form as so many tunes from the Great American Songbook — the 32-bar AABA form, in which each section is eight measures long. After 24 bars of introductory material, we settle into the heart of the song. Bars 25–32 and 33–40 are essentially identical. They are the A sections. Measures 41–48, in contrast, are based on a different harmonic progression, forming the B section, or bridge, then bars 49–56 return to the A section. All of this means, of course, that in practicing 16 bars of the music, you'll essentially be practicing 32. Two for the price of one! So, knowing the architecture of a song can be an invaluable tool for learning.

Another cool thing to note is the incorporation of a *blue note* — the lowered 7th — in this case a Bb on the C7 chord. This note was most likely inspired by African-American music, and the simple alteration lends a rather soulful quality to the song.

The Sound of Music (page 203)

The Sound of Music was the final collaboration of Richard Rodgers and Oscar Hammerstein II. With the book by Howard Lindsay and Russel Crouse, the musical was based on Maria von Trapp's *The Story of the Trapp Family Singers* (1949), a memoir by the former nun, and was also inspired by a pair of movies about the family — *Die Trapp-Familie* (1956) and *Die Trapp-Familie in Amerika* (1958). In the story, which is set in Austria, the postulant Maria finds that she's not cut out for a life of religious service, and she is sent to be the governess of the seven children of the widowed Captain Georg von Trapp. The two end up getting married, and following their honeymoon find Austria to have been invaded by the Nazis. Then, on the eve of World War II, the family escapes over the mountains into Switzerland.

The Sound of Music opened on Broadway on November 16, 1959, and ran for 1,443 performances. It was directed by Vincent J. Donehue and choreographed by Joe Layton, and the original cast included Mary Martin as Maria and Theodore Bikel as Captain Georg von Trapp. Although the show didn't exactly win rave reviews — one critic called it a "great step backward" for Rodgers and Hammerstein — it was well received by audiences and earned eight awards. The musical opened in London on May 18, 1961, and ran for 2,385 performances, and a 1965 film version starring Julie Andrews and Christopher Plummer helped cement the work as one of the most beloved of all musicals.

The title song of *The Sound of Music* is sung in Act I by Maria, and it is also considered one of the greatest songs in movie history. This is a very tender number, so it's important to play everything *legato,* or smooth and flowing. To do this most effectively, observe all the slurs, playing the notes without separation.

 Starting in the refrain, you'll see some upstemmed, cue-size notes. Although these phrases are optional, they have an interesting function, echoing the vocal melody two beats later and an octave higher. You might first try learning the arrangement without these notes, adding the imitative phrases only once you have the main parts down.

The song contains a lot of lovely harmonies. Especially striking is the E/F chord — an E triad (E–G#–B) with an F in the bass. Although an E chord on its own sounds pretty plain, with the note F, which is distantly related to the chord, it sounds exotic. This makes the song more interesting — if you substitute a diatonic chord like D minor (D–F–A) for the E/F, you can clearly hear the difference.

Sunrise, Sunset (page 216)

The storyline of *Fiddler on the Roof,* which features music by Jerry Bock, lyrics by Sheldon Harnick, and a book by Joseph Stein, is based on *Tevye and His Daughters* (1894), by Sholem Aleichem, a popular Yiddish writer and humorist. *Fiddler* is a loving and sometimes painful depiction of the everyday life, joys, and travails of a Czarist-era Russian Jewish milkman and his family, which includes five strong-willed daughters.

The original Broadway production of the show was directed and choreographed by Jerome Robbins, and featured Zero Mostel as Tevye, the philosophical milkman, and Beatrice Arthur as Golde, his cynical but loving wife. It opened on September 22, 1964, and ran for 3,242 performances, making it the first Broadway musical to pass the 3,000 mark. It won nine Tony Awards, and for every dollar invested in it earned a staggering $1,574. The show has been revived a number of times on Broadway, with such noteworthy performers as Chaim Topol (who also starred in the 1971 film adaptation), Theodore Bikel, Leonard Nimoy, and Alfred

Molina all playing Tevye. Perhaps the most bizarre revival was produced in 2006, in which Harvey Fierstein and Rosie O'Donnell were cast in the lead roles.

One of many memorable tunes generated by *Fiddler,* the stately waltz "Sunrise, Sunset" is a poignantly beautiful expression of the everyday sentiment ("Children grow up too fast") and has for more than 40 years been a staple of the wedding-band repertoire. This stately waltz is arranged here in the key of G minor. Throughout, remember to count "*One*-two-three," and so on, adding a little emphasis to the downbeat of each measure, and making sure to cut off most of the bass notes after beat 1, to make the music sound crisp and rhythmic. "Sunrise, Sunset" is a moderately slow waltz, so avoid the temptation to rush as you move along.

Although "Sunrise, Sunset" is largely diatonic, notice some F♯s here and there. This note comes from the G harmonic minor scale (G–A–B♭–C–D–E♭–F♯), which can be thought of as the G natural minor scale (G–A–B♭–C–D–E♭–F), with a raised 7th (F♯). The harmonic minor scale lends an exotic sound to the piece. Try playing bar 6 with an F♮ instead of an F♯, and hear that the music sounds comparatively plain without this accidental.

The Surrey with the Fringe on Top *(page 220)*

Oklahoma! was the first show written by the team of Richard Rodgers and Oscar Hammerstein II. It helped develop the form of the musical from a loose collection of humorous sketches into a cohesive story told with songs and dances, designed to evoke a wide range of emotions. And more than any previous musical, it contained musical motifs that occurred throughout, providing structural integrity. Originally titled *Away We Go, Oklahoma!,* the musical was based on the 1931 Lynn Riggs play *Green Grow the Lilacs.* Set in 1906 on the Indian territory now known as Oklahoma, it tells the story of a romance between a cowboy, Curly McLain, and a farmer girl, Laurey Williams, and of the jealous farmhand, Jud Fry, who challenges their love.

Directed by Rouben Mamoulian, the original Broadway production opened on March 31, 1943 and ran for a record-breaking 2,212 performances. Whereas most musicals had previously used actors who happened to have vocal abilities, Rodgers and Hammerstein did the opposite, so the musical featured a little-known cast including Alfred Drake as Curly, Joan Roberts as Laurey, and Howard Da Silva as Jud Fry. One of the first postwar musicals to hit London, *Oklahoma!* opened on the West End on April 30, 1947, running for 1,543 performances, and several revivals followed between 1951 and 2002. Also, in 1955, the musical was made into a film, which starred Gordon MacRae, Shirley Jones, and Rod Steiger. The movie won Academy Awards for Best Sound and Best Score.

Heard in Act I, "The Surrey with the Fringe on Top" is one of the most well-known songs from *Oklahoma!* In the number, Curly attempts to persuade Laurey to go to a social with him in a deluxe vehicle. In cut time, "Surrey" has a danceable two-step feel, emphasizing the upbeat. Like in country music, the simple bass line falls on beats 1 and 3 and sticks mostly to chord roots, hitting the fifth when a chord is held for an extended time, as in the first several measures of the refrain. Be sure to render the bass line in a lively even manner — think of swinging your partner to and fro.

They Say It's Wonderful *(page 230)*

One of the most prolific of all American composers, Irving Berlin was one of only a small handful of Broadway songwriters who wrote both music and lyrics. Berlin composed over 3,000 songs and many of them, such as "God Bless America" and "White Christmas," have had a profound impact on American culture. He wrote 21 Broadway scores. His most successful was *Annie Get Your Gun* (1946), produced by Richard Rodgers and Oscar Hammerstein II. Legend has it that Berlin was asked to write the music after the original composer, Jerome Kern, died suddenly. At first, Berlin denied the job, claiming to be ignorant about "hillbilly" music, but he soon acquiesced, and the original Broadway production, starring Ethel Merman and Ray Middleton, opened on Broadway on May 16, 1946 and ran for 1,147 performances. The show also had a long run in London, spawning numerous revivals, as well as film and television versions.

The story behind *Annie Get Your Gun* is a fictionalized version of an Ohio sharpshooter, Annie Oakley (1860–1926). In the musical, a traveling Wild West Show comes into town, and Annie quickly falls in love with the show's sharpshooter, Frank Butler. She joins the show so she can win the affections of Frank, who is actually in search of a more feminine woman. Annie is further hindered by the fact that she can shoot better than Frank, but in the end, she lets him win the contest. He falls in love with her and they get married.

One of the most popular songs from the musical, "They Say It's Wonderful" has been covered by everyone from Tony Bennett to John Coltrane to Frank Sinatra, and was even sung by actress Kirsten Dunst in *Spider-Man 3*. The song is a sweet and melodic ballad, so be sure to play it slowly, gently, and with expression, but be careful not to overdo it and risk sounding melodramatic.

Played in the key of F major, the song is packed with fancy jazz chords and substitutions. What is a substitution? For example, starting eight bars before the first ending (on the syllable "grand"), you'll find an Am–A♭m6–Gm9 progression. Normally, the ear would expect to hear some type of D chord in between the Am and Gm9 chords, but the A♭m6 chord adds a nice chromatic flavor and smoothly connects the chords by half step. Not to be too technical, but in jazz, this is known as *tritone substitution*. The A♭m6 chord sits in for a D-type chord; the roots of these two chords are a tritone apart, hence the name.

'Til Him *(page 225)*

The Producers (1968) was the first film written and directed by Mel Brooks, the great American writer, actor, comedian, and producer. Years later, Brooks was convinced to turn his movie into a musical. Something of a Renaissance man, he ended up writing the lyrics himself, the music with Glen Kelly, and the book with Thomas Meehan. Set in New York in 1959, the story tells of two questionable musical theater producers, Max Bialystock and Leo Bloom, who try to get rich by putting on what is sure to be a Broadway flop — *Springtime for Hitler: A Gay Romp with Adolf and Eva at Berchtesgaden,* by Franz Liebkind. Naturally, things get complicated when the show actually ends up being successful.

Directed and choreographed by Susan Stroman, the original Broadway production of *The Producers* opened on April 19, 2001 and ran for 2,502 performances. It starred Nathan Lane as Max Bialystock and Matthew Broderick as Leo Bloom. And with its raucous humor, parodying homosexuals and Nazis, the show won 12 Tony Awards, surpassing *Hello, Dolly!,* which in 1964 earned 10. Meanwhile, the London production opened on November 9, 2004, starring Lane again, and Lee Evans as Leo Bloom. Following several other successful tours and productions, *The Producers* was adapted into a film in 2005, featuring most of the original Broadway cast. And the show even found itself on a television program, HBO's *Curb Your Enthusiasm,* when in most of Season Four, Larry David and Ben Stiller were starring in a production of the musical.

"'Til Him" is sung by Leo and Max near the end of Act II. The song's structure is interesting. Following a four-bar intro, Leo sings in F major for 34 bars. After that, Max takes over in E major for 16 bars, then goes back to F for eight bars before finally joining with Leo. If you compare the sections, notice that much of the music is similar. The first bar of Max's entrance, for instance, is basically the same as Leo's, except transposed to E. Seeing how a song's sections are similar helps you learn everything more quickly.

Till There Was You (page 234)

Meredith Willson was an American composer and playwright whose complex yet subtle music appealed to both classical and mass audiences. Willson's best-known songs include "Seventy-Six Trombones," "It's Beginning to Look Like Christmas," and "Till There was You." His best-known musical, for which he wrote not only the music but also the book and lyrics, was *The Music Man*. In the story, "Professor" Harold Hill is a con man who convinces parents he can teach their children to become promising musicians. He collects money for instruments and uniforms, then skips town before he can be caught. However, in the fictional town of River City, Iowa, Harold becomes drawn to the librarian, Marian Paroo, who catches on to him. He chooses to stay and face the music and in the end is rewarded as parents cheer on his new boys' band.

Following years of conception, more than 40 drafts, and a change of producers, *The Music Man* finally opened on Broadway on December 19, 1957. Running for 1,375 performances, it was directed by Morton DaCosta and choreographed by Onna White. The original cast included Robert Preston as Harold Hill and Barbara Cook as Marian. It won a Tony Award for Best Musical, has enjoyed a couple of revivals, and was made into a motion picture in 1962 (starring Preston once again). In 2003 a television movie was made starring Matthew Broderick as Hill and Kristin Chenoweth as Marian.

"Till There Was You" is sung by Marian to Harold near the end of Act II. It was also a big hit for the Beatles, in 1963. Played in the key of E♭ major, the song achieves much of its jazzy flavor through diminished 7th chords. A cool thing about these voicings is how smoothly they connect with chords that are fully within the key. For example, between the E♭maj7 and Edim7 chords, only two notes change — the root is raised a half step, to E, and the 7th is lowered a half step, to D♭. In fancy music terminology, this is known as smooth *voice leading*. Another interesting choice of harmony is the A♭m6 chord, which is borrowed from the key of E♭ minor for a striking sound.

A couple of things to look out for — on the last page of the music, eight bars from the first ending, note that the left hand ventures way up to the treble clef on beats 2 and 3. And in the next measure is an octave sign *(8va)*, which is used for ease of reading; simply play the bracketed notes an octave higher than indicated.

Tomorrow (page 240)

Annie, featuring music by Charles Strouse, lyrics by Martin Charnin, and a book by Thomas Meehan, is based on Harold Gray's *Little Orphan Annie,* a comic strip inspired by an 1885 poem by James Whitcomb Riley called "Little Orphant Annie." Set during the Great Depression in New York's Lower East Side, the musical follows Annie as she escapes from a vile orphanage run by the wicked Miss Hannigan and sets out on an unsuccessful quest to find her birth parents. But things work out for Annie when she starts a new life with a generous millionaire, Daddy Warbucks.

The original Broadway production of the musical opened on April 21, 1977 and ran for a total of 2,377 performances. It starred Andrea McArdle (Annie), Reid Shelton (Daddy Warbucks), and Dorothy Loudon (Miss Hannigan) and won seven Tony Awards, including Best Musical. McArdle, who was succeeded on Broadway by a young Sarah Jessica Parker, also starred in the enormously successful 1978 London production of the show.

"Tomorrow," Annie's great signature song, is an enduring pop culture phenomenon as demonstrated by the fact that it is featured in the 1993 hit film *Addams Family Values.* Don't be intimated by the tune's tricky-looking rhythms. To learn them properly, take things slow and *subdivide* — feel the beat in small units. Start by counting "One-ee-and-uh, two-ee-and-uh, three-ee-and-uh, four-ee-and-uh," and so on. In the first bar, the 32nd-note B falls in between the "ee" and the "and" of "one," the eighth-note C falls on the "and," and the last note of the measure falls on the "uh" of "four." In the second bar, on beat 2, the dotted-eighth C falls on the "ee," and on beat 3, the eighth-note F falls on the "ee" and the subsequent 16th-note F on the "uh." If you take the time to break rhythms down in this manner, you'll get to the point where you'll be able to play them automatically on sight, without having to think about how they're divided.

What I Did for Love (page 244)

With a book by James Kirkwood, Jr. and Nicholas Dante, lyrics by Edward Kleban, and music by Marvin Hamlisch, *A Chorus Line* is a tribute to Broadway's chorus dancers. Its plot was actually based on the events of several actual workshops with Broadway dancers. Featuring 19 main characters, the musical examines the emotional rollercoaster experienced every time these highly-skilled but typically underpaid performers show up for an audition.

Directed by Michael Bennett, who collaborated on the choreography with Bob Avian, *A Chorus Line* opened on Broadway on July 25, 1975, and ran for 6,137 performances — a record first eclipsed by *Cats,* in 1997, then by *The Phantom of the Opera,* in 2006. The original cast included Scott Allen, Kelly Bishop, Robert Lupone, Wayne Cilento, Ronald Dennis, and Baayork Lee. The show won 12 Tony Awards, including Best Musical, Best Actress, and Best Director. One of the few musicals to ever receive the Pulitzer Prize for Drama, it also won the New York Drama Critics' Circle Award for Best Play of the season. The show has been produced by countless high school, college, and dinner-theater groups, and a film adaptation, directed by Richard Attenborough, was released in 1985.

"What I Did for Love," the biggest hit to emerge from *A Chorus Line,* is arranged here in the key of C major. This slow and sensitive number contains a handful of complex chords, along with the occasional 16th-note run. To master this complexity more easily, try learning both hands slowly and separately, scanning ahead for those pesky accidentals and taking care to avoid playing choppily.

In bars 13 and 32, on beat 2, are some 32nd-note grace notes. Play these quickly and smoothly just before the beat, without disrupting the rhythmic flow of the piece. It might be a good idea to make sure that you have the whole right-hand part down before adding these dramatic flourishes. If they're too challenging to play, though, then simply omit the grace notes altogether. Also, heads up on the time change in bar 24 — again, without upsetting the flow of the piece, drop two beats before moving back to 4/4 in the ensuing measure.

Who Can I Turn To (When Nobody Needs Me) (page 237)

The British team of Leslie Bricusse and Anthony Newley hit it big with their 1962 musical *Stop the World — I Want to Get Off,* and they hoped to replicate that success three years later with *The Roar of the Greasepaint — The Smell of the Crowd.* An allegory about the seemingly eternal class struggle in Great Britain, the musical tells the story of the downtrodden Cocky, who is vanquished by the well-born Sir when the two compete in a comically drawn Game of Life.

During its initial tour, the musical didn't prove popular enough to make it to London's West End, but the American producer David Merrick was impressed enough by the show (and its low staging cost) to bring it to Broadway. *Greasepaint,* directed by Anthony Newley and choreographed by Gillian Lynne, opened there on May 16, 1965, with Anthony Newley (Cocky) and Cyril Ritchard (Sir) in the lead roles. The gamble paid off: The U.S. version was a success, running for 231 performances and earning six Tony nominations.

Heard in both Acts I and II, "Who Can I Turn To (When Nobody Needs Me)" is one of the musical's finest songs, and has been covered by vocalists like Tony Bennett (whose version of the tune, some say, contributed enormously to the show's Stateside success) and Dusty Springfield, as well as jazzers like pianist Bill Evans.

The song appears more difficult to play than is actually the case. It is based on a 32-bar AA form, which commences following a four-bar intro. This means that the first 16 bars (5–20) of the piece are nearly identical to the final 16 (21–26), so in mastering the first A section, you essentially learn the entire song. When working on that first section, be sure to take things slowly. To inject greater expressive *oomph* into your performance, try fiddling on your own with the dynamics. For example, you can gradually increase the volume as you play the first eight bars en route to the second set of eight.

A Wonderful Day Like Today *(page 252)*

"A Wonderful Day Like Today," from Leslie Bricusse and Anthony Newley's 1965 musical *The Roar of the Greasepaint — The Smell of the Crowd,* quickly became a standard and throughout the years has been interpreted by a number of singers, including Shirley Bassey, Lena Horne, and Johnny Mathis.

The song kicks off in 6/8, so remember to count "*One*-two-three, *four*-five-six," emphasizing the first and fourth beats while playing at a moderate tempo. Beginning in bar 5 of the verse, pairs of slanted parallel lines start to appear in the music. Called *caesuras,* these tell you to pause briefly. Throughout this section, be mindful of the slurs, as *legato* is crucial to playing this part effectively.

In contrast to the verse, the chorus moves to cut time, or 2/2, and here the dotted-eighth note of 6/8 should be roughly equivalent to the half note of the new time signature. When you get to that chorus, sit on the first two quarter notes (on the lyrics "On" and "a") for as long as you want, as indicated by the *fermatas,* and then, at the repeat sign, charge into brisk cut time and all those driving quarter notes.

Younger Than Springtime *(page 248)*

Following their smash hits *Oklahoma!* (1943) and *Carousel* (1945), Richard Rodgers and Oscar Hammerstein II achieved even greater success with the musical *South Pacific.* Produced by Rodgers and Hammerstein in association with Leland Hayward and Joshua Logan, the show opened on Broadway on April 7, 1949 and ran for 1,925 performances, earning nine million dollars. The 1958 film adaptation grossed more than 16 million dollars, at that time the sixth highest in the history of American movies; the sheet music and album also sold in record numbers. *South Pacific* played for two and a half years in London, after which the company went on a tour that lasted another year and a half, spawning several revivals. The musical received a number of prestigious awards, including the Pulitzer Prize for Drama, the New York Drama Critics Award, seven Antoinette Perry Awards, and nine Donaldson Awards.

The show combines the plot lines of two stories taken from James A. Michener's 1946 World War II collection, *Tales of the South Pacific.* Ensign Nellie Forbush, a U.S. Navy nurse from Arkansas, hooks up romantically with a middle-aged French plantation owner, Emile de Becque. At the same time, Lt. Cable, one of a group of restless U.S. Navy men hungry for female companionship, falls in love with Liat, the teenage daughter of a souvenir dealer. Ahead of its time, the musical deals with the racial tensions that inevitably resulted when American military personnel came in close contact with the indigenous populations in the South Pacific during the war.

"Younger Than Springtime," sung by Cable to Liat in Act I, is characterized by sudden dynamic and expressive shifts from section to section, so pay particularly close attention to the markings in the arrangement. Although the intro is loud (*f*), things become moderately quiet (*mp*) at bar 5. Really milk this and all such dramatic dynamic changes.

Note the striking changes in texture between sections in the tune. Before the refrain, for example, the melody is played in right-hand block chords, with a rhythmic pattern of quarter note-half-quarter in the bass. At the refrain, however, the melody is played with single notes in the right hand, while the left-hand accompaniment is made from straight quarter notes on top of whole notes. This sort of change in texture helps keep the listener's attention.

Memory

from CATS
Music by Andrew Lloyd Webber
Text by Trevor Nunn after T.S. Eliot

Mid - night. _____ Not a sound from the pave - ment. _____ Has the moon lost her
Mem - ory _____ all a - lone in the moon - light _____ I can smile at the

mem - ory? _____ She is smil - ing a - lone. _____ In the
old days, _____ I was beau - ti - ful then. _____ I re -

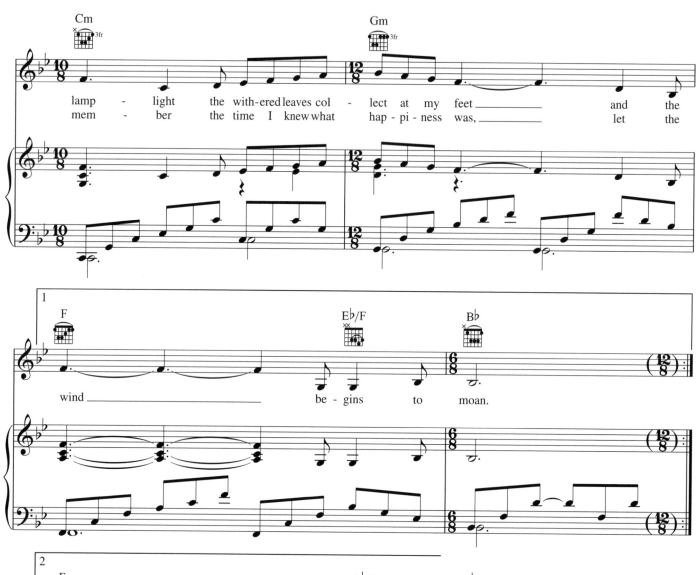

lamp - light the with-ered leaves col - lect at my feet _____ and the
mem - ber the time I knew what hap - pi - ness was, _____ let the

wind _____ be - gins to moan.

mem - ory live a - gain.

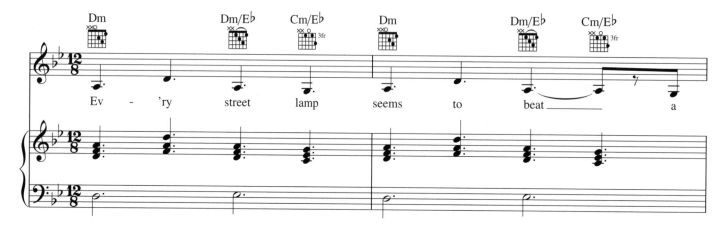

Ev - 'ry street lamp seems to beat _____ a

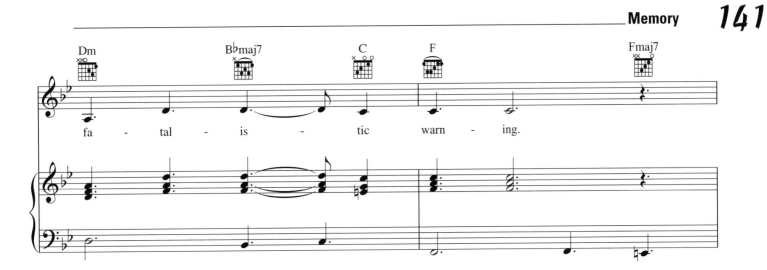

fa - tal - is - tic warn - ing.

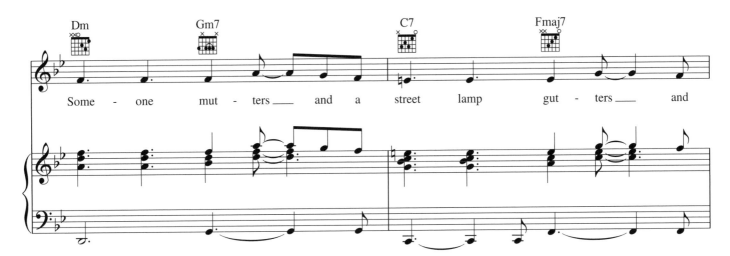

Some - one mut - ters ___ and a street lamp gut - ters ___ and

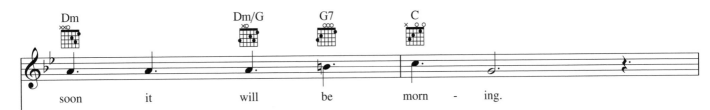

soon it will be morn - ing.

rit.

Day - light. ___ I must wait for the sun - rise, ___ I must think of a

a tempo

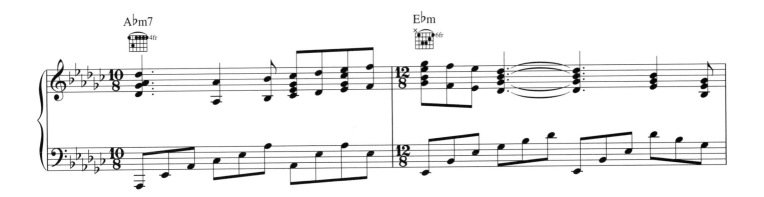

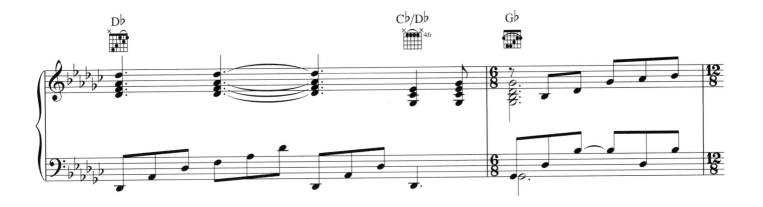

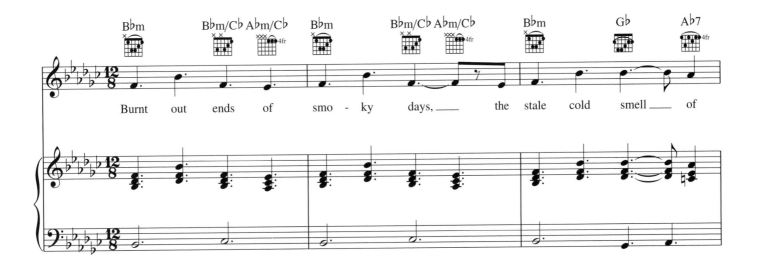

Burnt out ends of smo - ky days, ___ the stale cold smell ___ of

morn - ing. ____ The street lamp dies, an - oth - er

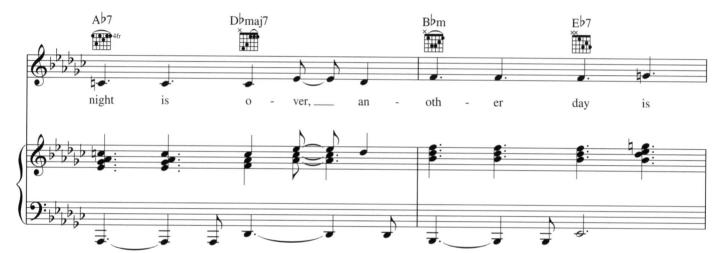

night is o - ver, ____ an - oth - er day is

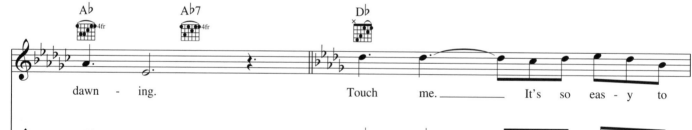

dawn - ing.

rit.

Touch me. ____ It's so eas - y to

a tempo

leave me ____ all a - lone with the mem - ory ____ of my days in the

rall.

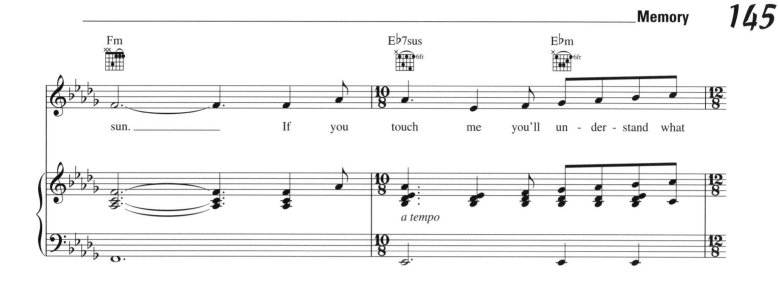

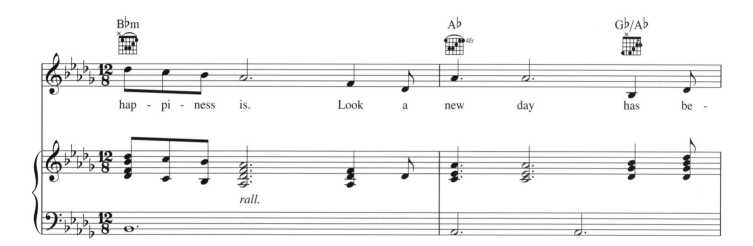

Mama, I'm A Big Girl Now

from HAIRSPRAY
Music by Marc Shaiman
Lyrics by Marc Shaiman and Scott Wittman

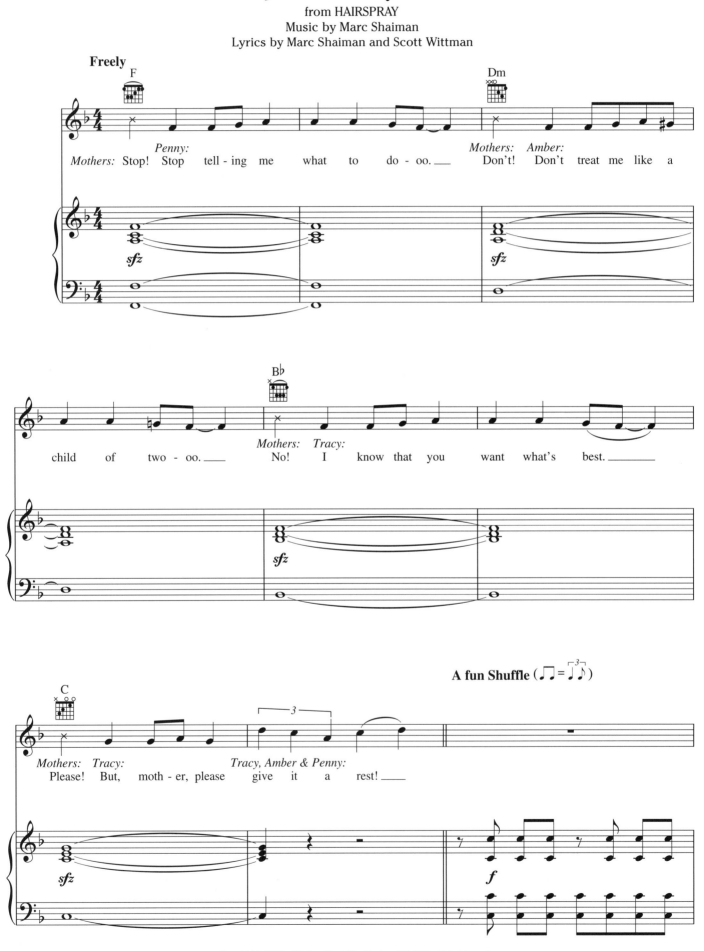

Mothers: Stop!   Don't!   No!   Girls: Please! _____   Mothers: Stop!   Don't!

No!   Girls: Please! _____   Mothers: Stop!   Don't!   No!   Girls: Please! _____

Ma-ma, I'm a big girl   now!   Tracy: Once up-on a time when I was

just a   kid, _____   you nev-er let me do just what the old-er kids did. ____   But

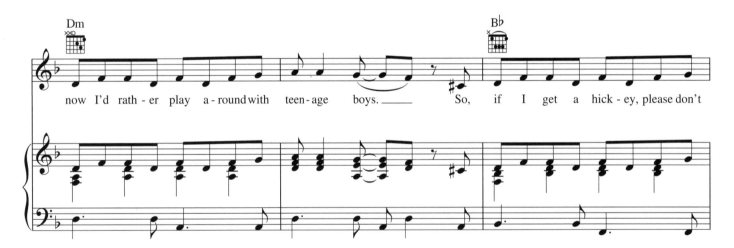

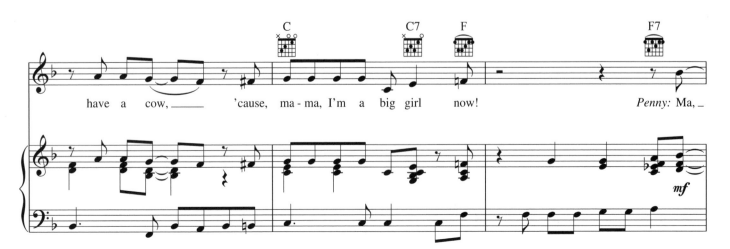

I gotta tell you that with-out a doubt I get my best danc-ing les-sons from you-

-oo.___ You're ___ the one who taught me how to "Twist and Shout" ___ be-cause you

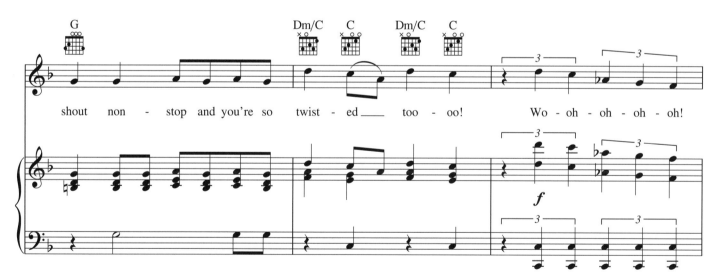

shout non - stop and you're so twist-ed ___ too - oo! Wo - oh - oh - oh - oh!

Tracy: Once I used to fid-get 'cause I just sat home. ___ *Amber:* But now I'm just like Gid-get and I

got - ta get to Rome! *Penny:* So, say ar - ri - ve - der - ci! Too - dle - oo! And ciao! __ *Girls:* 'Cause,

ma - ma, I'm a big girl now! *All:* Oh - oh - oh! Stop! Don't!

No! Please! __ Stop! Don't! No! Please! __

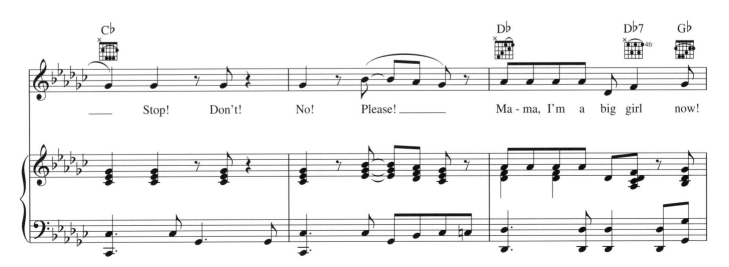

__ Stop! Don't! No! Please! __ Ma - ma, I'm a big girl now!

Chorus: Hey, ma - ma, say, ma - ma. *Tracy:* Once up-on a time I was a shy young thing. Could

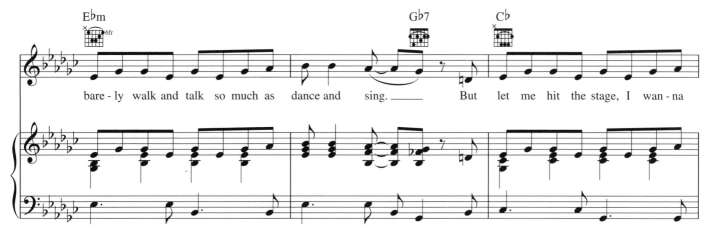

bare - ly walk and talk so much as dance and sing. But let me hit the stage, I wan-na

take my bow, 'cause, ma-ma, I'm a big girl now! *Amber:* Wo - oh - oh - oh - oh!

Once up-on a time I used to dress up "Ken," but now that I'm a wom-an I like

big - ger men! __ And I don't need a Bar - bie doll to show me how, ___ 'cause,

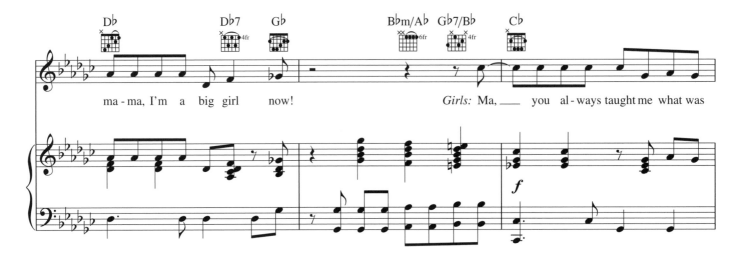

ma - ma, I'm a big girl now! *Girls:* Ma, ___ you al - ways taught me what was

right from wrong, and now I just wan - na give it a try - y. ___ Ma -

- ma, I've been in the nest for far too long. __ So please give a push and, ma - ma,

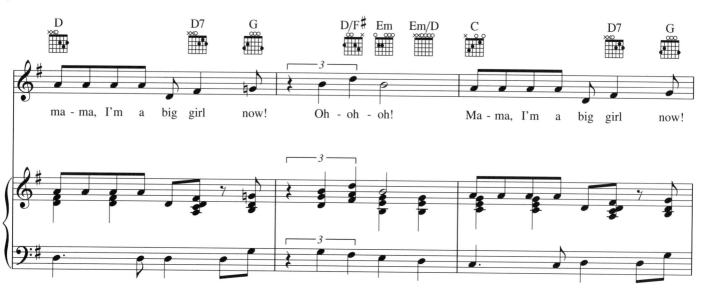

ma - ma, I'm a big girl now! Oh - oh - oh! Ma - ma, I'm a big girl now!

Amber: Hey - hey - hey - hey - hey! *Girls:* Ma - ma, ___ I'm a big girl!

Amber: Ooh, such a big, big girl! I'm a big girl now! ___

All: Stop! Don't!

Mamma Mia

from MAMMA MIA!
Words and Music by Benny Andersson, Bjorn Ulvaeus and Stig Anderson

look and I for-get ev-'ry-thing, ____ oh, ____ oh. ____

Mam-ma Mi-a, here I go a-gain. ____

G   C/G   G   D/G   D

My,   my   how ____ can I re-sist ya?

G   C/G   G

Mam-ma Mi-a, does it show a-gain, _ my, my, just _

how much I've missed ya? Yes, ___ I've been bro - ken - heart - ed,

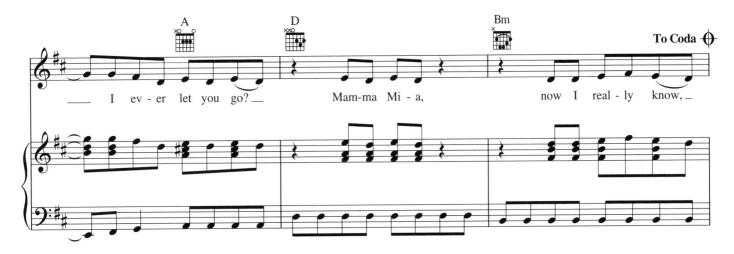

blue ___ since the day ___ we part - ed. Why, why did ___

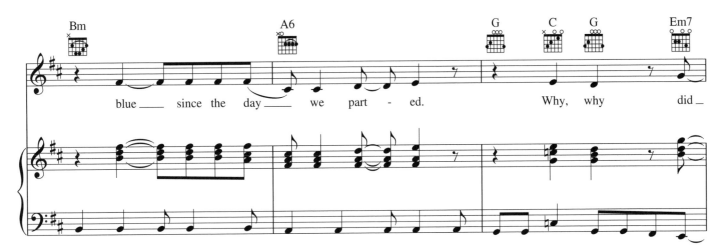

___ I ev - er let you go? ___ Mam-ma Mi - a, now I real - ly know, ___

my, my, I _____ should not have let you go. ___

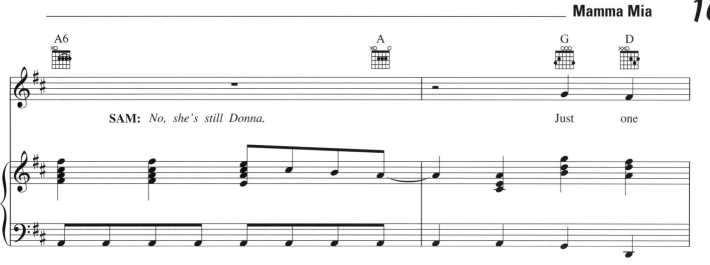

SAM: *No, she's still Donna.*   Just one

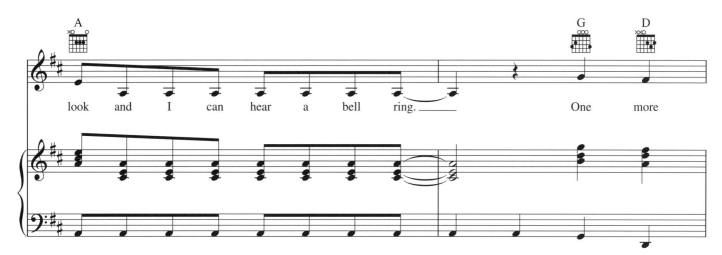

look and I can hear a bell ring._____   One more

look and I for-get ev-'ry-thing,_____   oh,_____ oh._____

D.S. al Coda

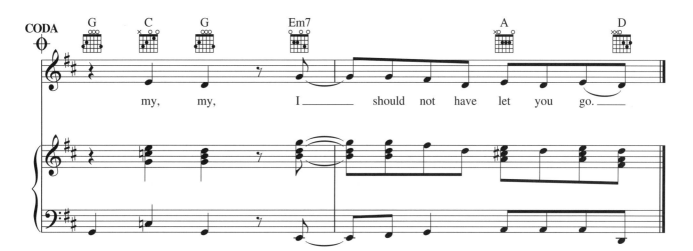

CODA

my, my,   I_____ should not have let you go._____

My Romance

from JUMBO
Words by Lorenz Hart
Music by Richard Rodgers

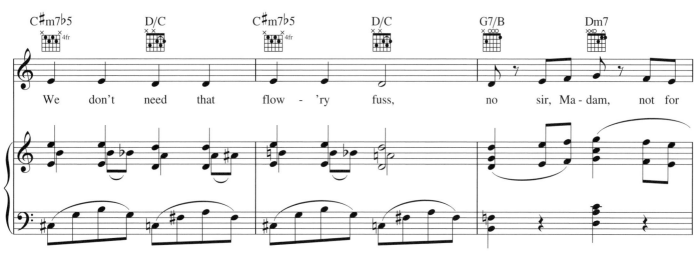

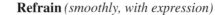

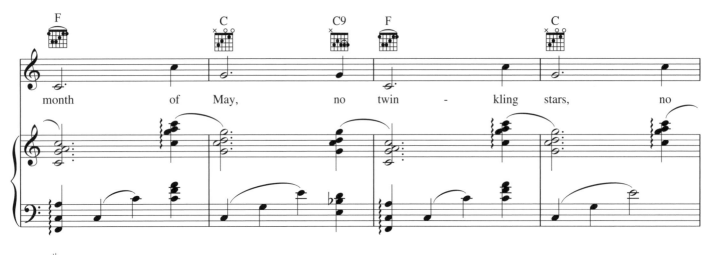

month of May, no twin - kling stars, no

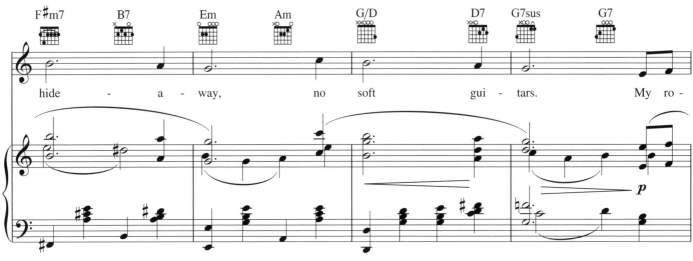

hide - a - way, no soft gui - tars. My ro -

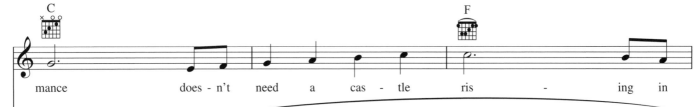

mance does - n't need a cas - tle ris - ing in

Spain, nor a dance to a con - stant - ly sur -

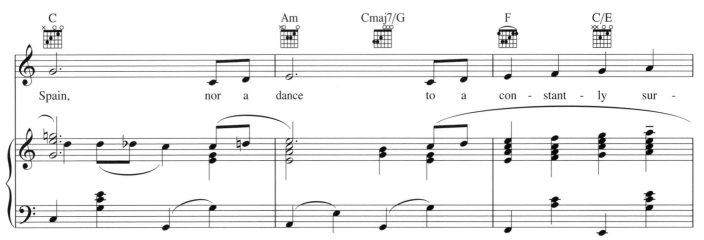

Ol' Man River

from SHOW BOAT
Lyrics by Oscar Hammerstein II
Music by Jerome Kern

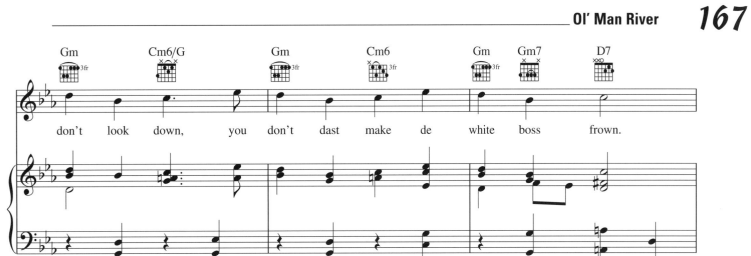

don't look down, you don't dast make de white boss frown.

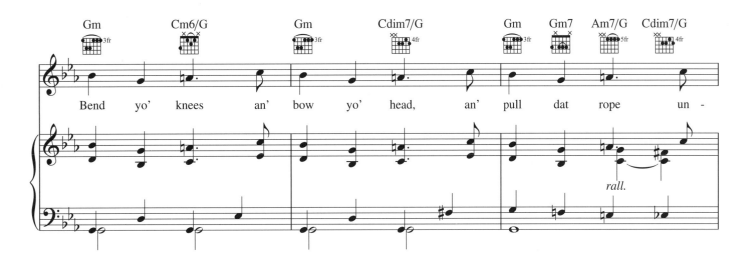

Bend yo' knees an' bow yo' head, an' pull dat rope un-

rall.

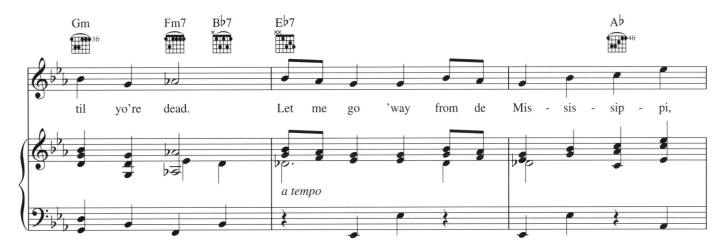

til yo're dead. Let me go 'way from de Mis - sis - sip - pi,

a tempo

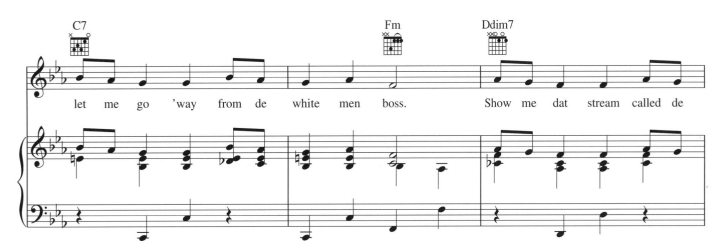

let me go 'way from de white men boss. Show me dat stream called de

riv - er Jor - dan. Dat's de ol' stream dat I long to cross. _____

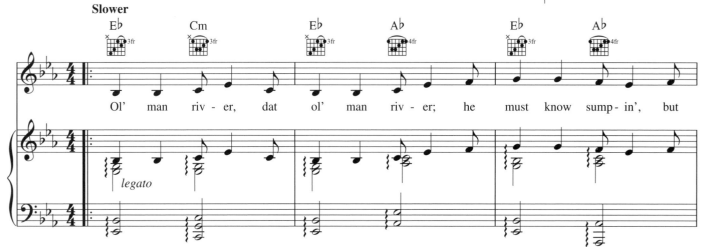

Ol' man riv - er, dat ol' man riv - er; he must know sump - in', but

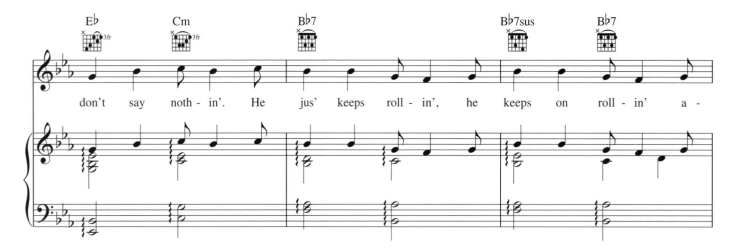

don't say noth - in'. He jus' keeps roll - in', he keeps on roll - in' a -

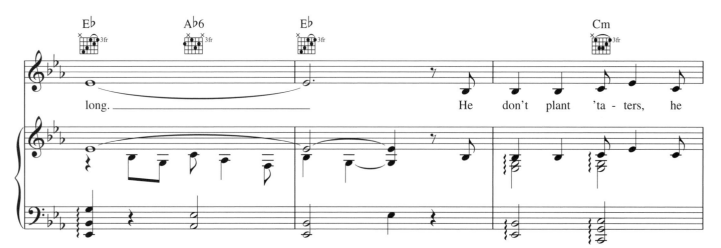

long. _____ He don't plant 'ta - ters, he

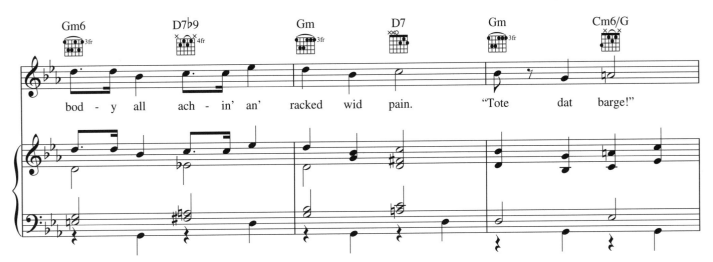

"Lift dat bale," Git a lit - tle drunk an' you land in jail.

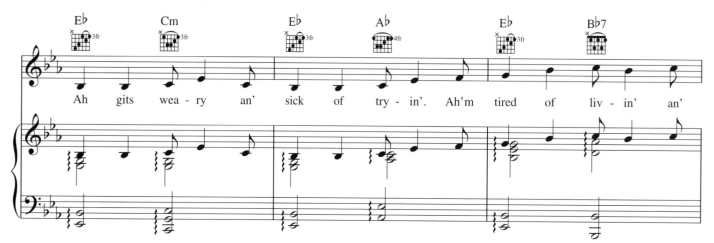

Ah gits wea - ry an' sick of try - in'. Ah'm tired of liv - in' an'

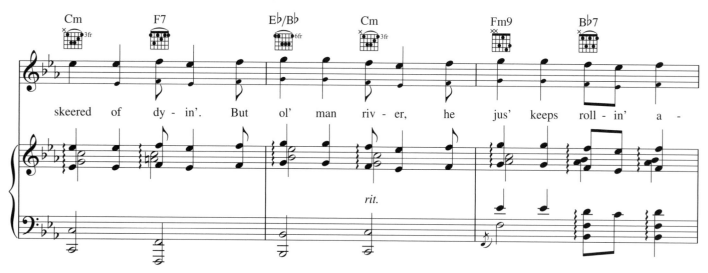

skeered of dy - in'. But ol' man riv - er, he jus' keeps roll - in' a -

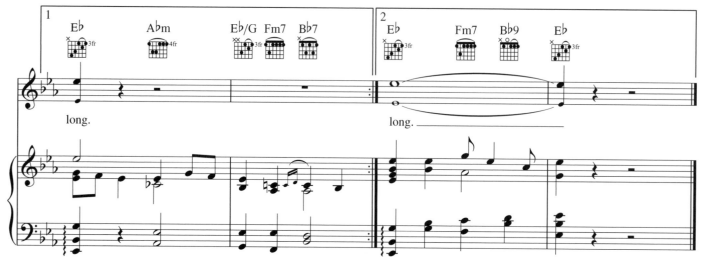

long.

long.

On The Street Where You Live

from MY FAIR LADY
Words by Alan Jay Lerner
Music by Frederick Loewe

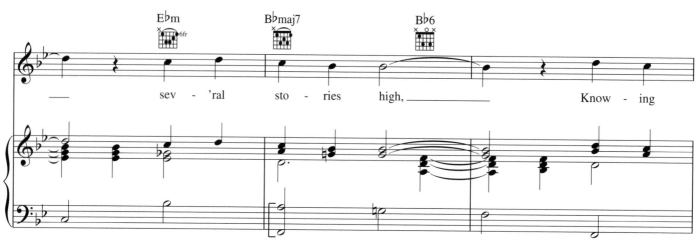

sev - 'ral   sto - ries   high, _____   Know - ing

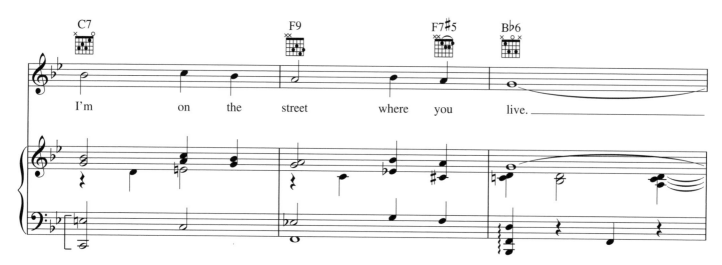

I'm   on   the   street   where   you   live. _____

___ Are   there   li - lac   trees _____   in   the

heart   of   town? _____   Can   you   hear   a   lark   in

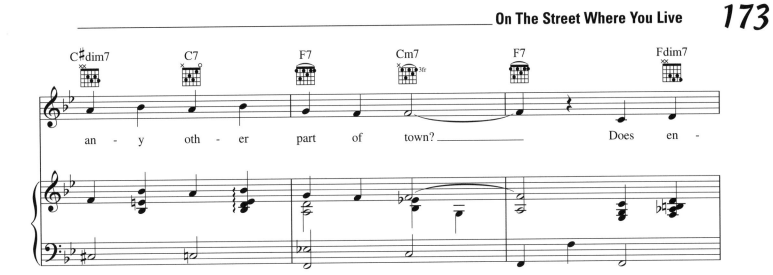

an - y oth - er part of town? _____ Does en -

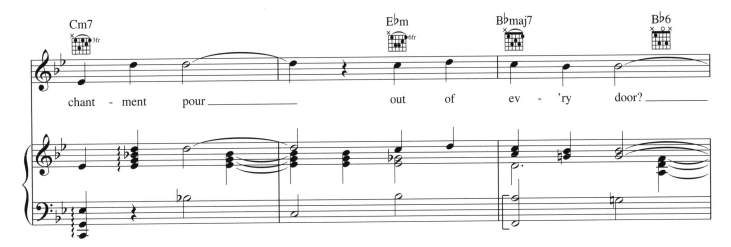

chant - ment pour _____ out of ev - 'ry door? _____

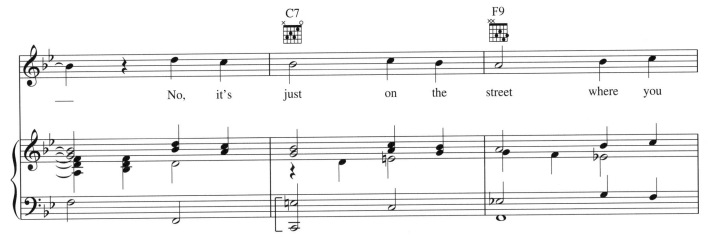

No, it's just on the street where you

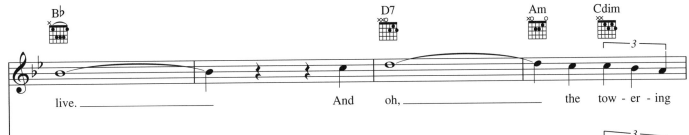

live. _____ And oh, _____ the tow - er - ing

On A Clear Day (You Can See Forever)

from ON A CLEAR DAY YOU CAN SEE FOREVER
Words by Alan Jay Lerner
Music by Burton Lane

clear day _____ how it will as - tound you _____

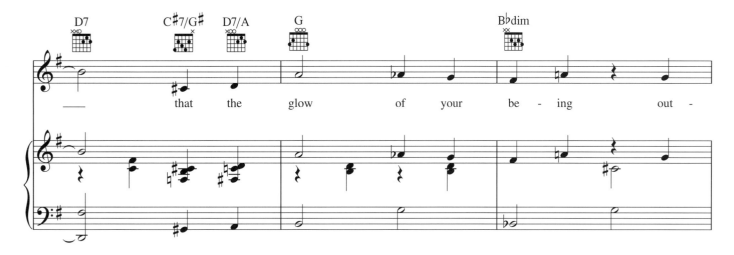

_____ that the glow of your be - ing out -

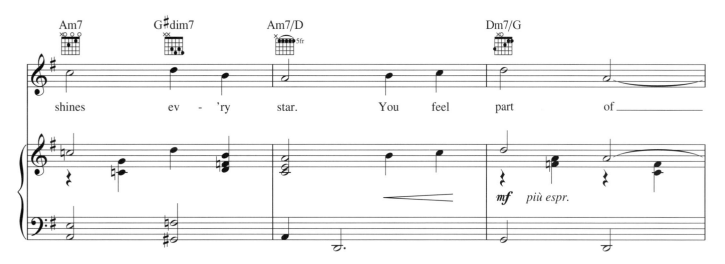

shines ev - 'ry star. You feel part of _____

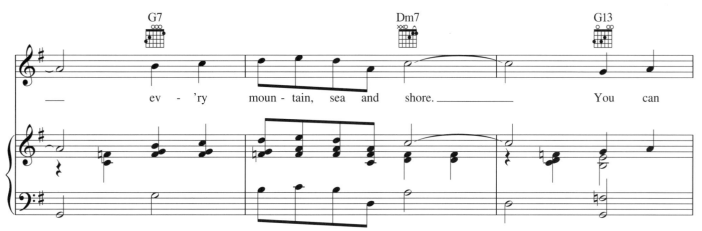

_____ ev - 'ry moun - tain, sea and shore. _____ You can

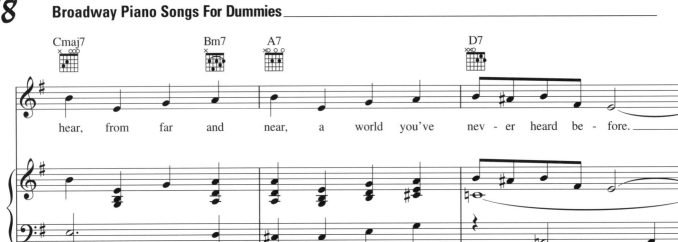

hear, from far and near, a world you've nev-er heard be-fore. _____

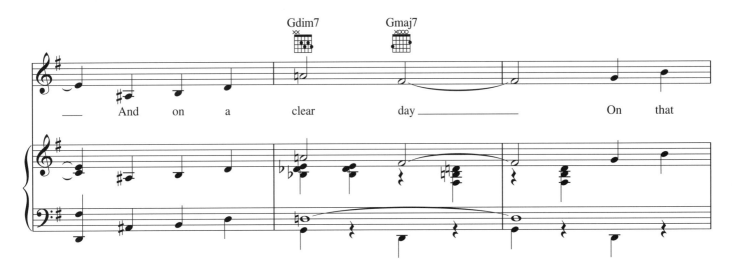

_____ And on a clear day _____ On that

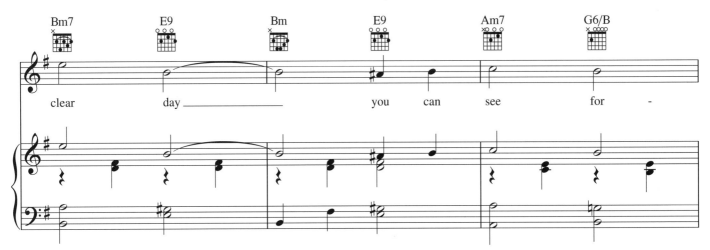

clear day _____ you can see for -

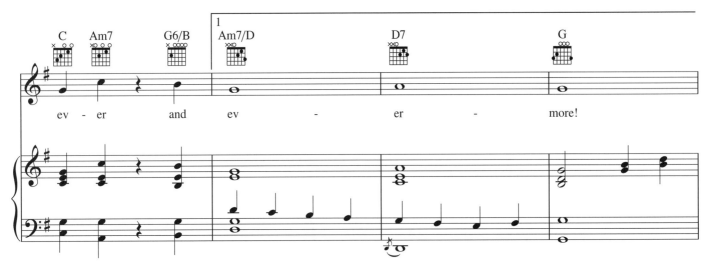

ev - er and ev - er - more!

Popular

from the Broadway Musical WICKED
Music and Lyrics by Stephen Schwartz

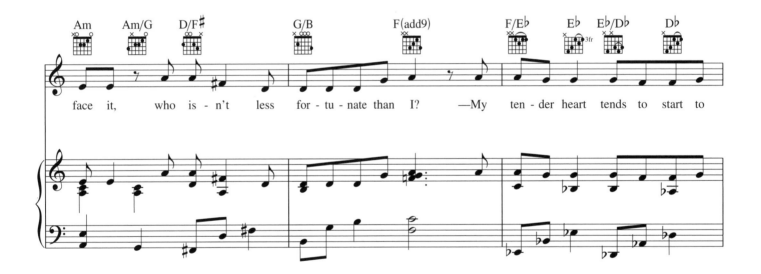

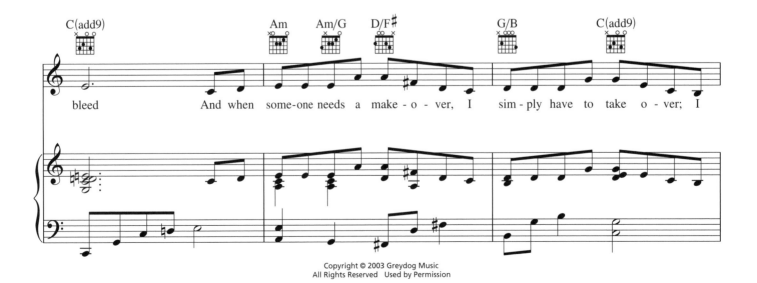

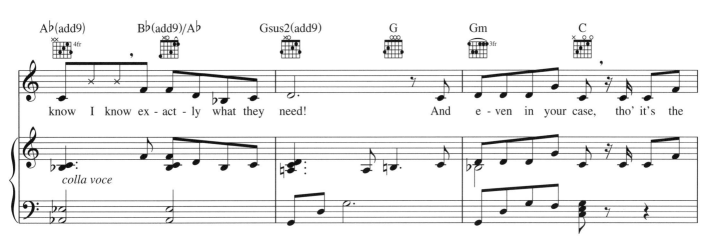

know I know ex - act - ly what they need! And e - ven in your case, tho' it's the

colla voce

tough - est case I've yet to face, ___ don't wor - ry, I'm de - ter - mined to suc -

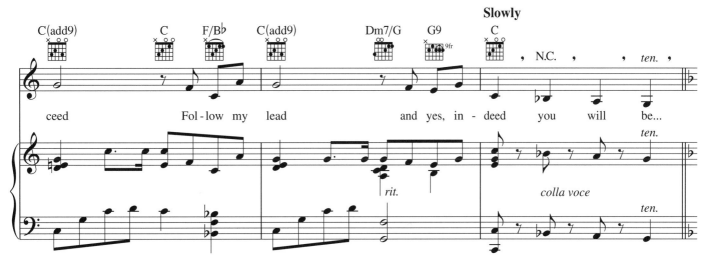

ceed   Fol - low my lead   and yes, in - deed   you   will   be...

rit.   _colla voce_

Bright and bubbly

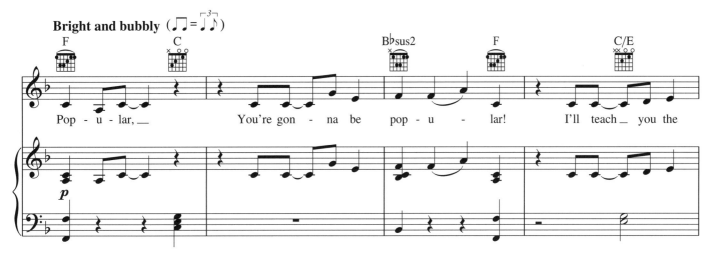

Pop - u - lar, ___   You're gon - na be pop - u - lar!   I'll teach _ you the

_p_

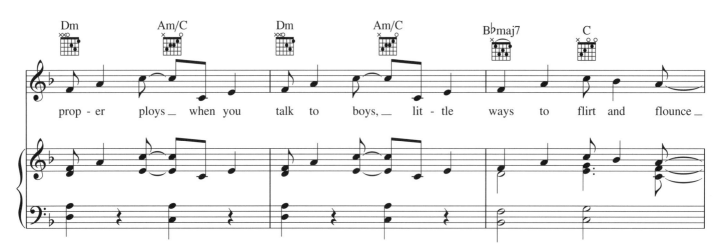

proper ploys __ when you talk to boys, __ lit-tle ways to flirt and flounce __

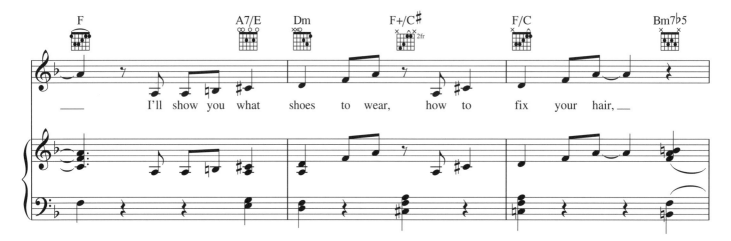

__ I'll show you what shoes to wear, how to fix your hair, __

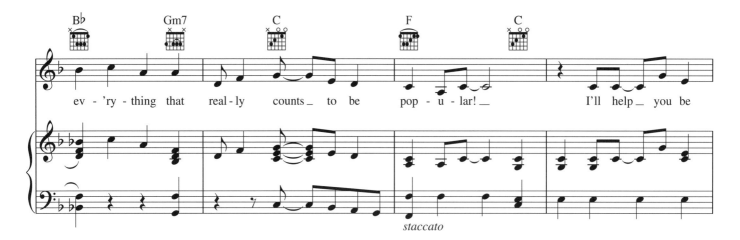

ev-'ry-thing that real-ly counts __ to be pop-u-lar! __ I'll help __ you be

staccato

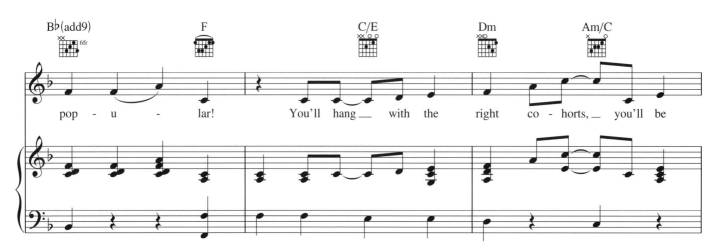

pop-u-lar! You'll hang __ with the right co-horts, __ you'll be

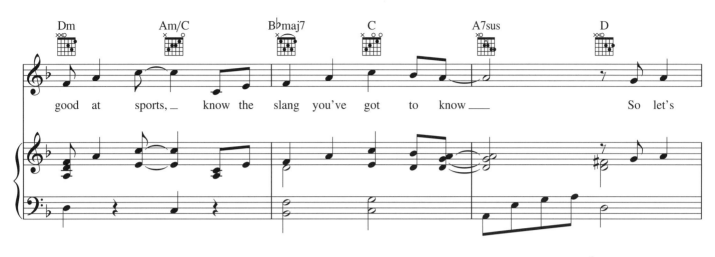

good at sports,__ know the slang you've got to know __ So let's

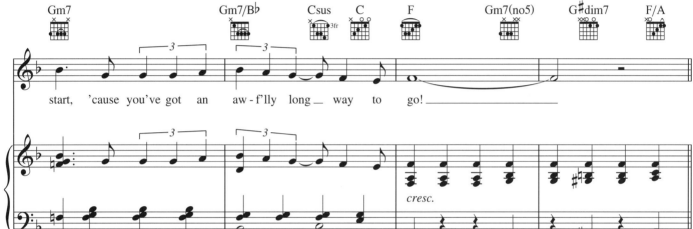

start, 'cause you've got an aw-f'lly long__ way to go! _____

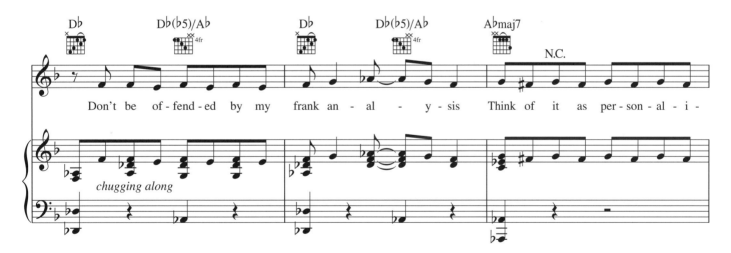

Don't be of-fend-ed by my frank an-al-y-sis Think of it as per-son-al-i-

chugging along

ty di-al-y-sis Now that I've cho-sen to be-come a pal,__ a sis-

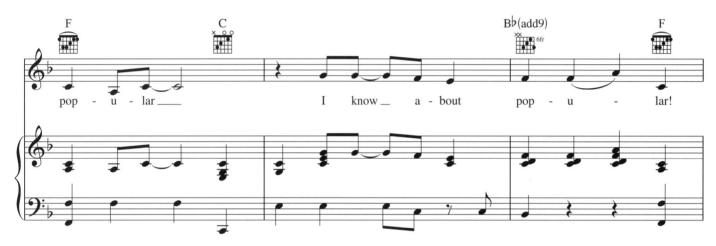

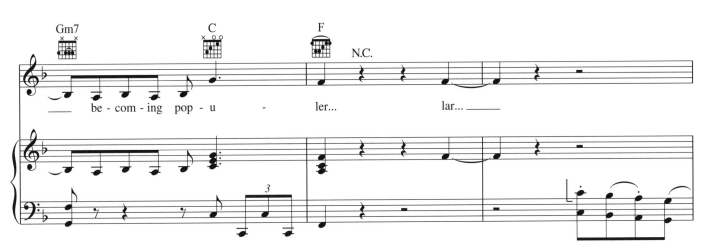

be - com - ing pop - u - ler... lar...

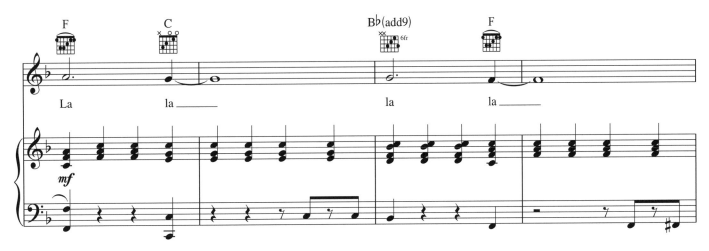

La la la la

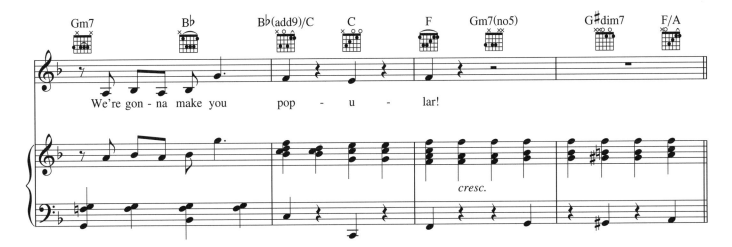

We're gon - na make you pop - u - lar!

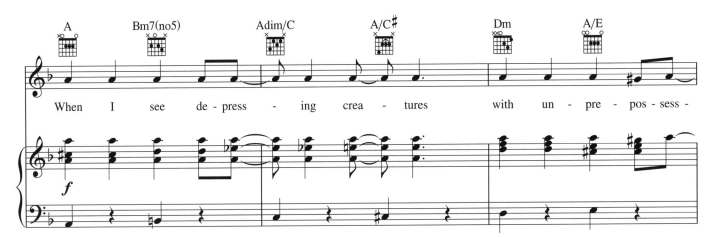

When I see de - press - ing crea - tures with un - pre - pos - sess -

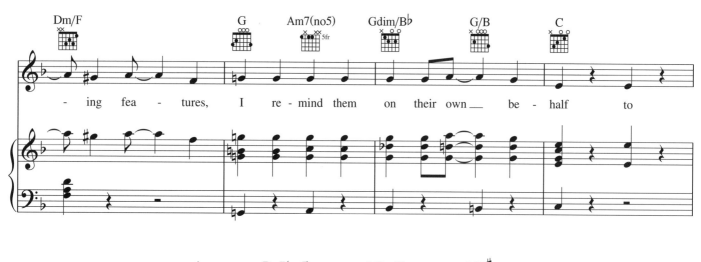

-ing fea - tures, I re - mind them on their own __ be - half to

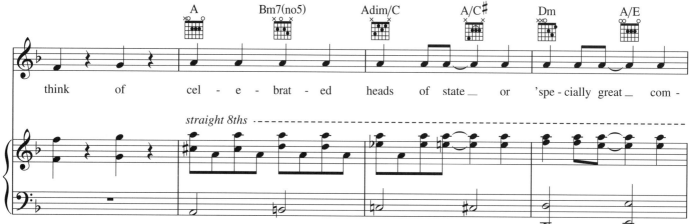

think   of   cel - e - brat - ed   heads   of   state __ or   'spe - cially great __ com -

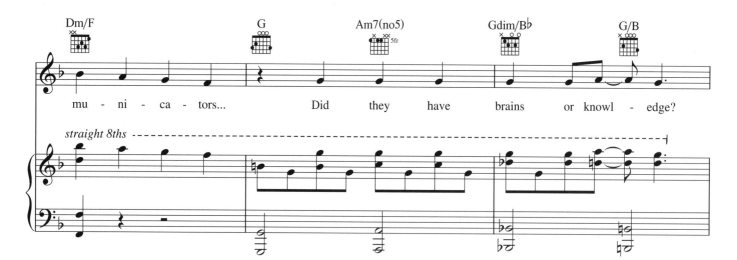

mu - ni - ca - tors...   Did   they   have   brains   or   knowl - edge?

Don't   make   me   laugh!   They   were   pop - u - lar __ Please!   It's   all __ a - bout

pop - u - lar! It's not ___ a - bout ap - ti - tude, ___ it's the

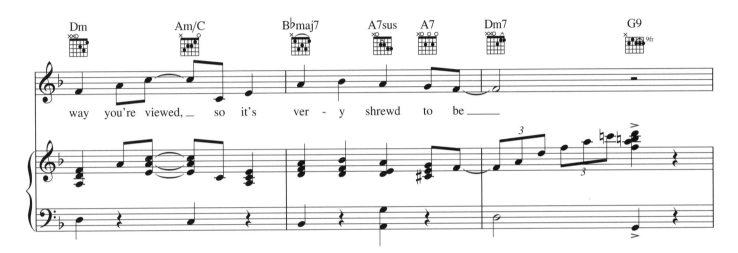

way you're viewed, ___ so it's ver - y shrewd to be ___

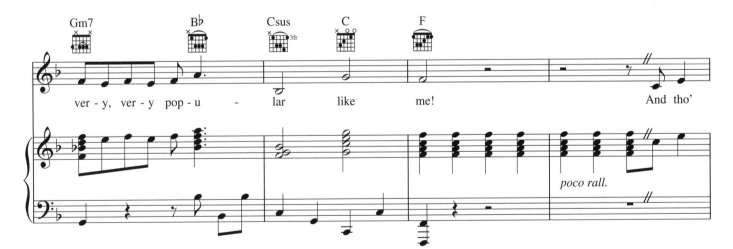

ver - y, ver - y pop - u - lar like me! And tho'

poco rall.

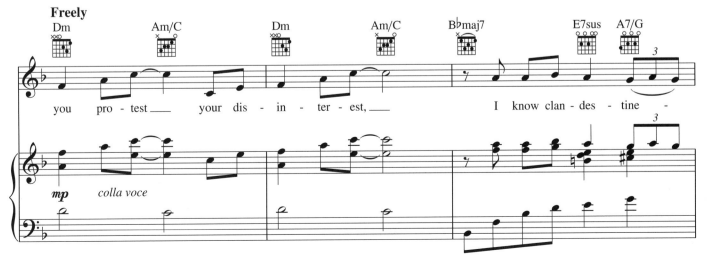

you pro - test ___ your dis - in - ter - est, ___ I know clan - des - tine -

mp *colla voce*

Freely

ly   You're gon-na grin and bear it   your new-found pop-u-lar-it -

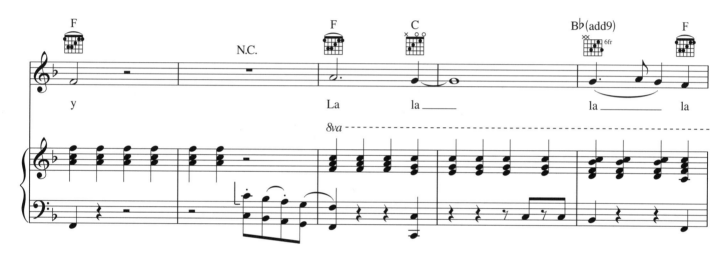

y   La   la _____   la _____ la

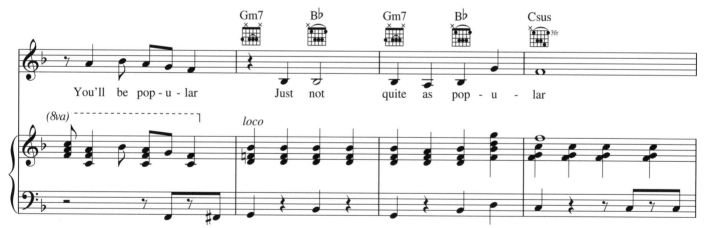

You'll be pop-u - lar   Just not   quite as pop-u - lar

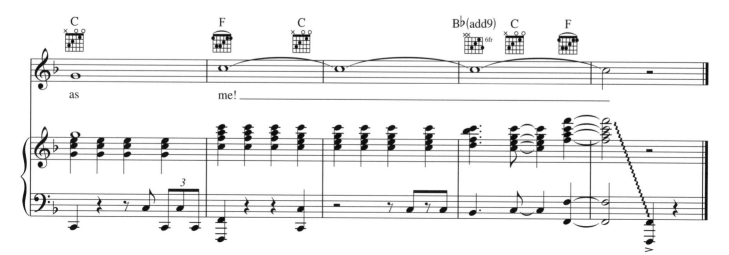

as   me! _____

Put On A Happy Face

from BYE BYE BIRDIE

Lyric by Lee Adams   Music by Charles Strouse

mask of trag - e - dy,   it's not your style;

You'll look so good that you'll be glad __ ya' de - cid - ed to smile! __

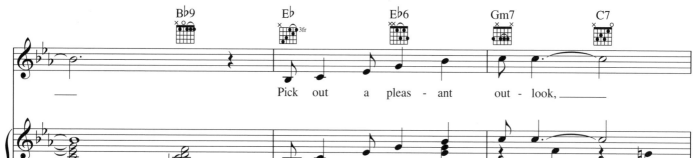

__   Pick out a pleas - ant out - look, _____

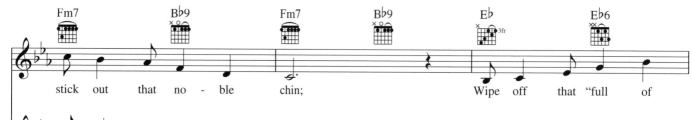

stick out that no - ble chin;   Wipe off that "full of

Real Live Girl

from LITTLE ME
Music by Cy Coleman
Lyrics by Carolyn Leigh

Moderate Waltz

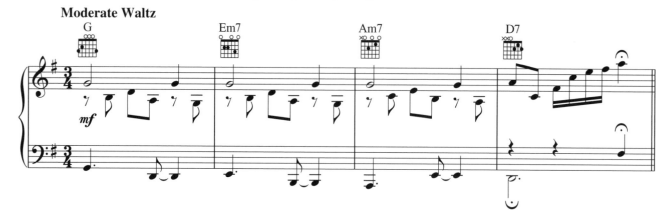

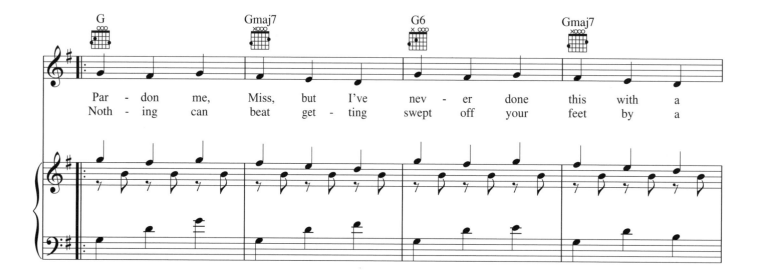

Par - don me, Miss, but I've nev - er done this with a
Noth - ing can beat get - ting swept off your feet by a

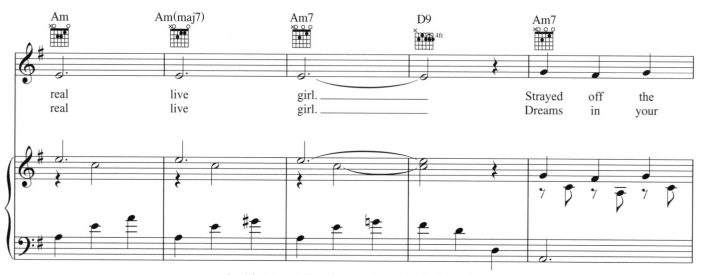

real live girl. _____
real live girl. _____
Strayed off the
Dreams in your

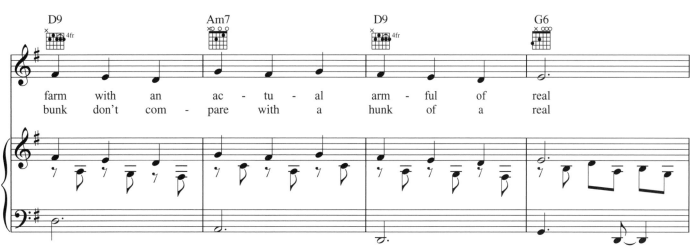

farm with an ac - tu - al arm - ful of real
bunk don't com - pare with a hunk of a real

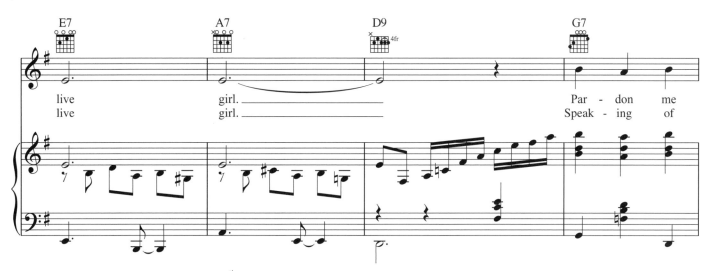

live girl. _____
live girl. _____

Par - don me
Speak - ing of

if your af - fec - tion - ate squeeze fogs up my
mir - a - cles, this must be it just when I

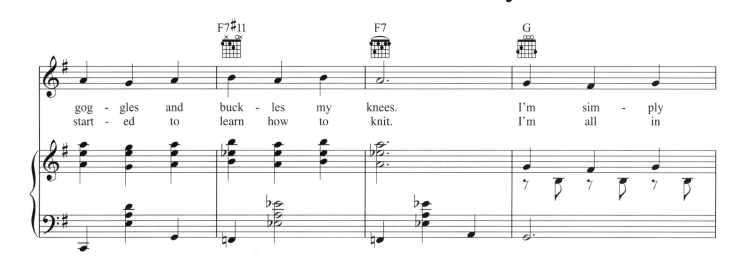

gog - gles and buck - les my knees. I'm sim - ply
start - ed to learn how to knit. I'm all in

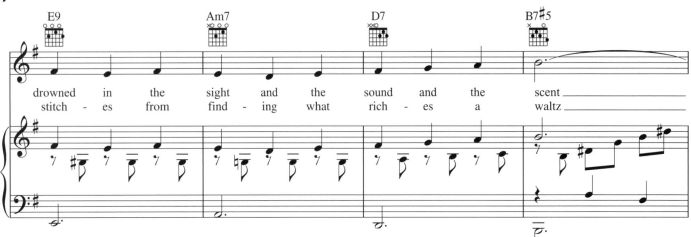

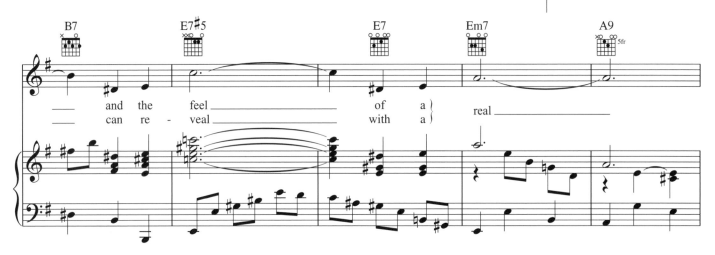

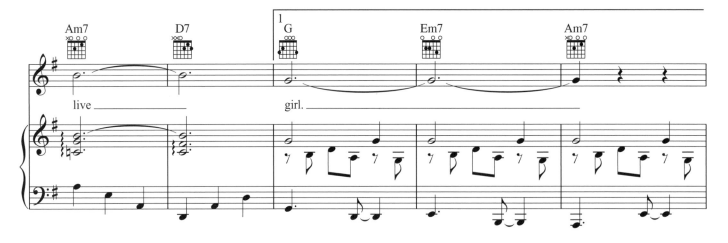

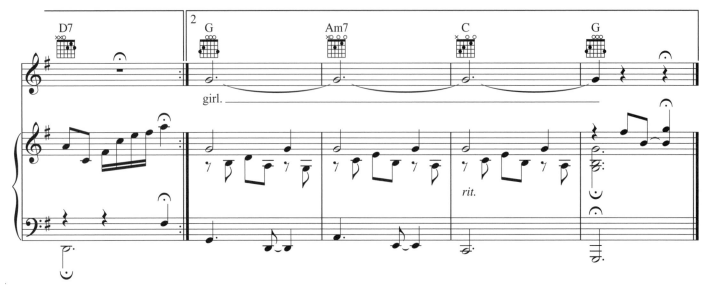

Satin Doll

from SOPHISTICATED LADIES
Words by Johnny Mercer and Billy Strayhorn
Music by Duke Ellington

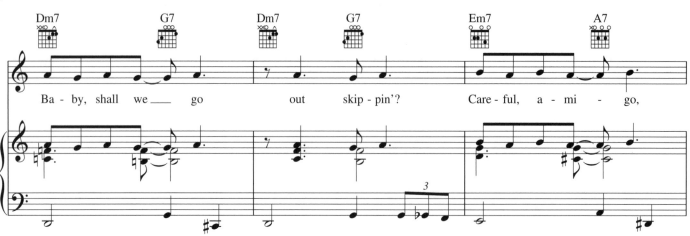

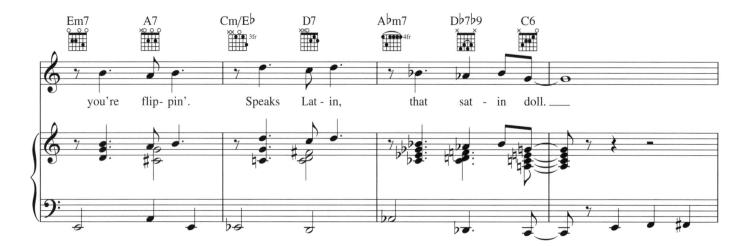

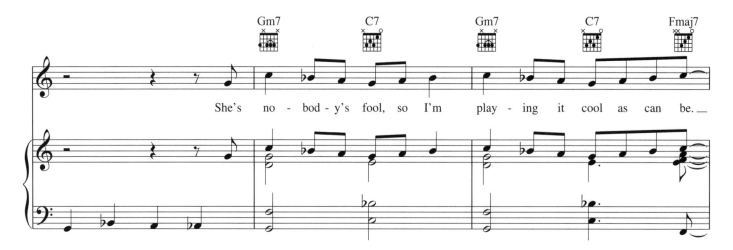

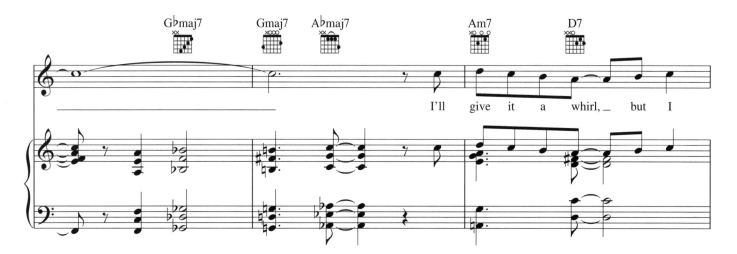

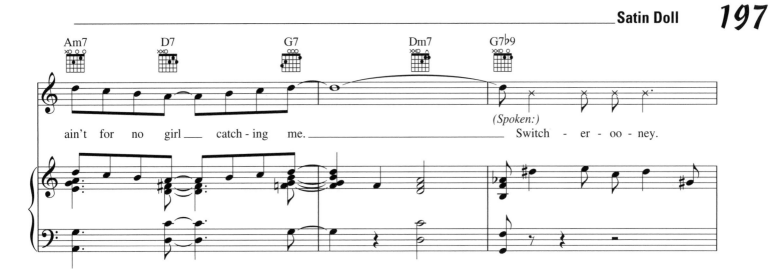

ain't for no girl___ catch-ing me.___ *(Spoken:)* Switch - er - oo - ney.

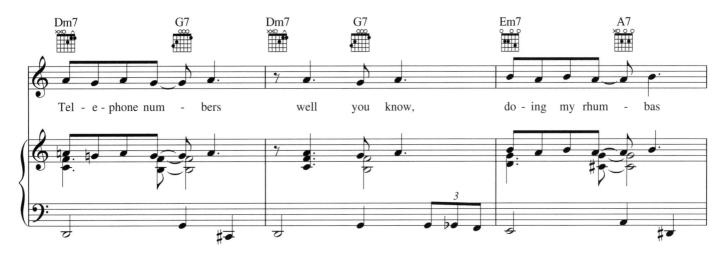

Tel - e - phone num - bers well you know, do - ing my rhum - bas

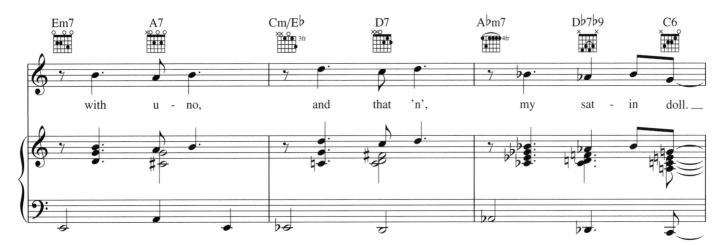

with u - no, and that 'n', my sat - in doll. ___

Seasons Of Love

from RENT

Words and Music by Jonathan Larson

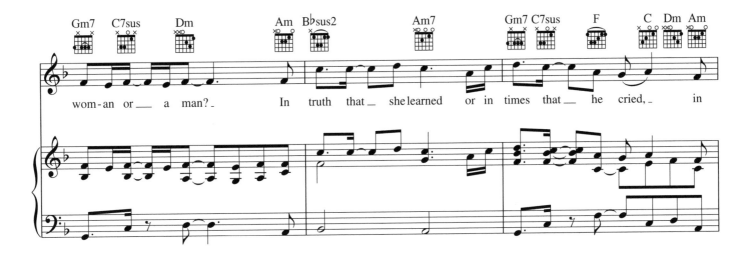

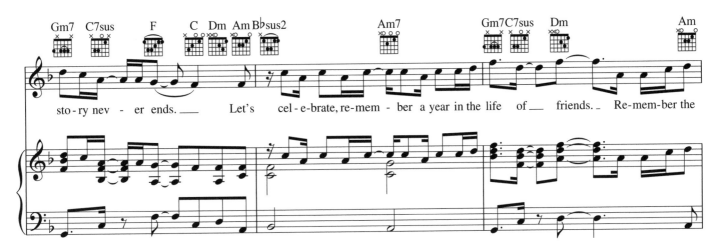

The Sound Of Music

from THE SOUND OF MUSIC
Lyrics by Oscar Hammerstein II
Music by Richard Rodgers

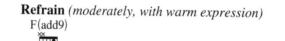

The hills fill my heart with the sound of mu - sic.

My heart wants to sing ev - 'ry song it hears.

My heart wants to beat like the wings of the birds that rise from the lake to the

trees. My heart wants to sigh like a chime that flies from a church on a

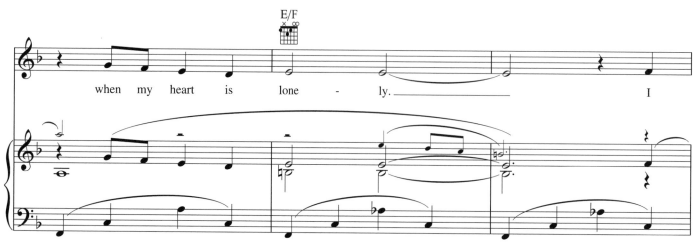

She Loves Me

from SHE LOVES ME
Words by Sheldon Harnick
Music by Jerry Bock

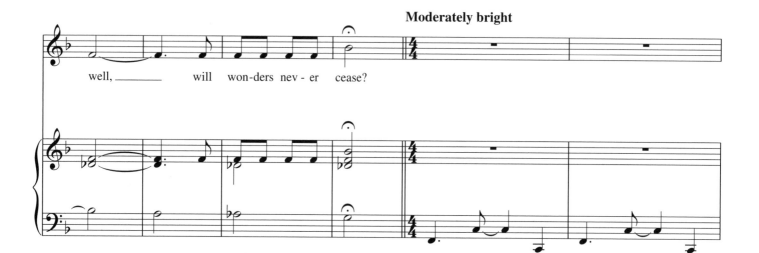

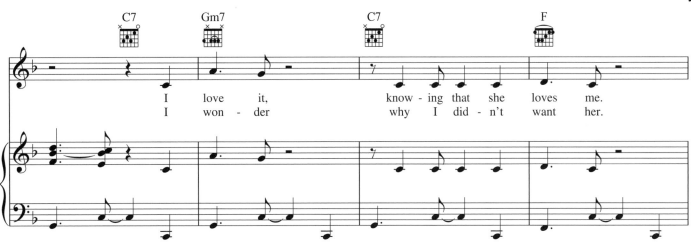

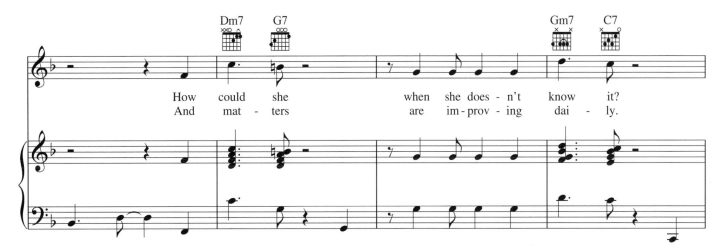

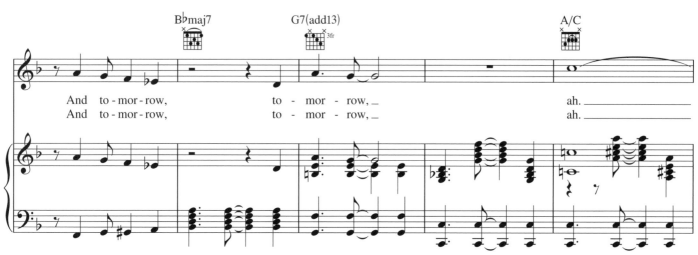

And to-mor-row,   to - mor - row, _   ah. _____
And to-mor-row,   to - mor - row, _   ah. _____

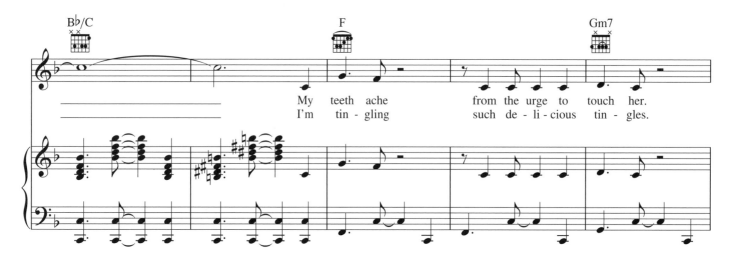

_____
_____   My   teeth ache   from the urge to   touch her.
      I'm tin - gling   such de - li - cious   tin - gles.

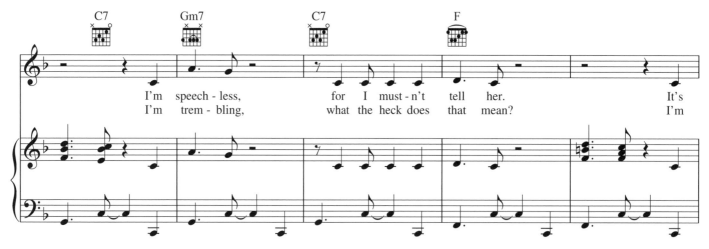

I'm   speech - less,   for I must - n't   tell   her.   It's
I'm   trem - bling,   what the heck does   that   mean?   I'm

wrong   now,   but   it won't be   long   now. _   Be -
freez - ing,   that's be - cause it's   cold   out. _   But

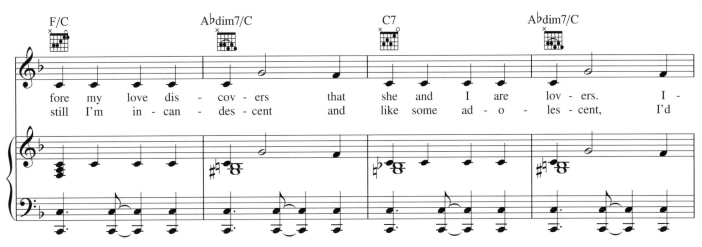

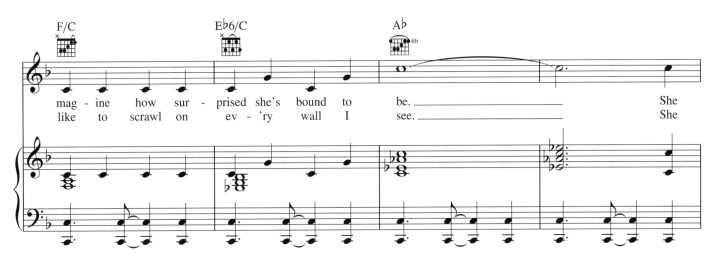

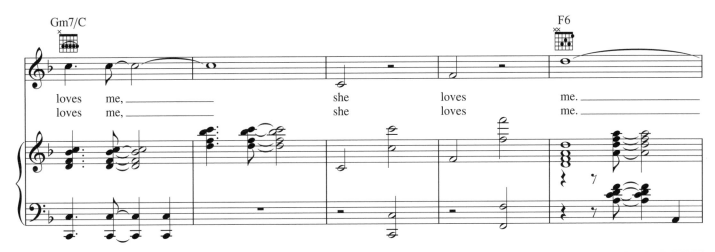

Somebody Loves Me

from GEORGE WHITE'S SCANDALS OF 1924
Words by B.G. DeSylva and Ballard MacDonald
Music by George Gershwin
French Version by Emelia Renaud

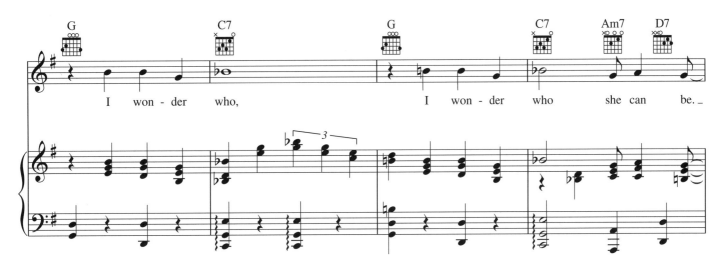

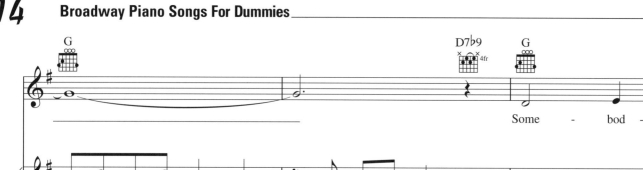

Some - bod - y

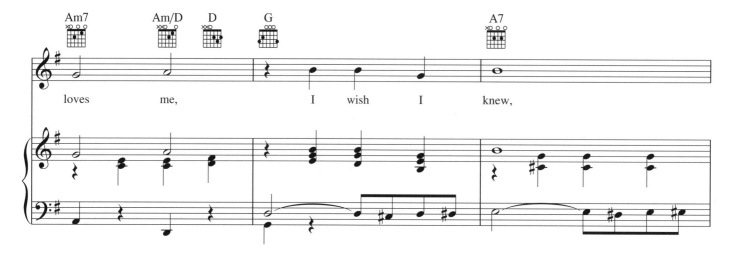

loves   me,   I   wish   I   knew,

who   can   she   be   wor - ries   me. _____

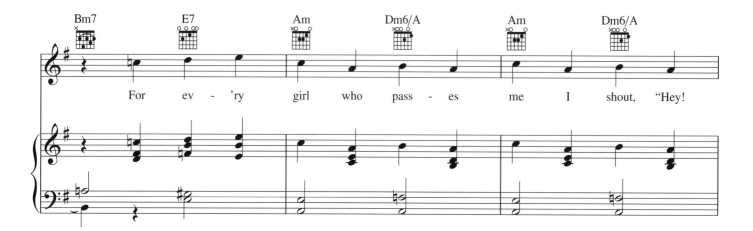

For   ev - 'ry   girl   who   pass - es   me   I   shout,   "Hey!

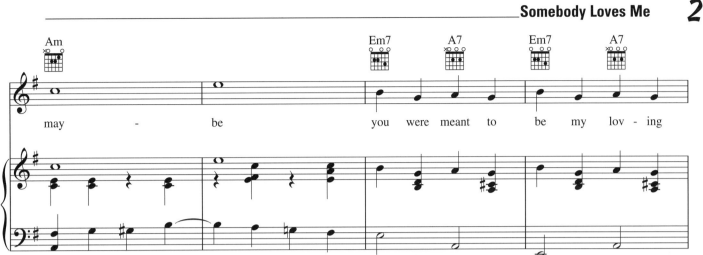

may - be ... you were meant to be my lov - ing

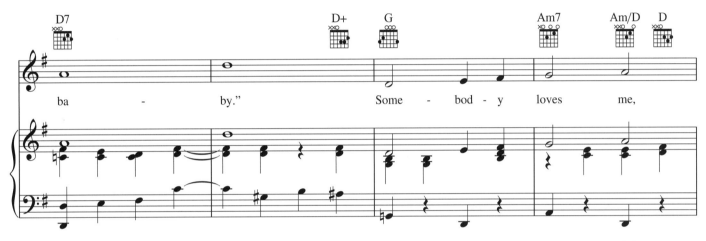

ba - by." Some - bod - y loves me,

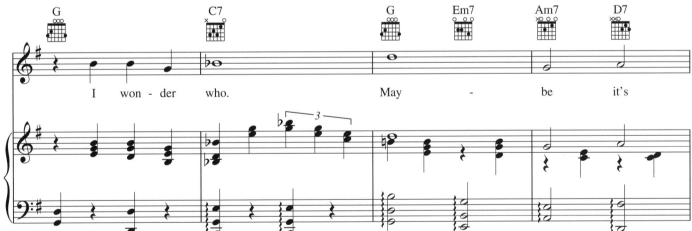

I won - der who. May - be it's

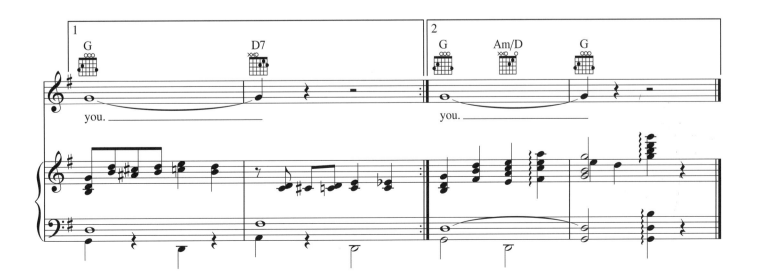

you. _____ you. _____

Sunrise, Sunset

from the Musical FIDDLER ON THE ROOF
Words by Sheldon Harnick
Music by Jerry Bock

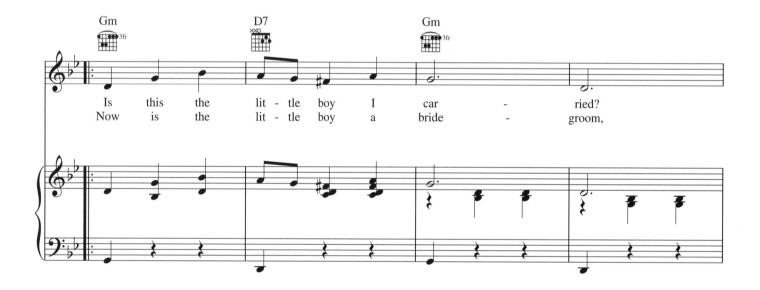

Is this the lit - tle boy I car - ried?
Now is the lit - tle boy a bride - groom,

Is this the lit - tle girl at play?
now is the lit - tle girl a bride?
I don't re -
Un - der the

mem-ber grow - ing old - er, when did
can-o-py I see them, side by

they? _____ When did she get to be a beau -
side. _____ Place the gold ring a-round her fin -

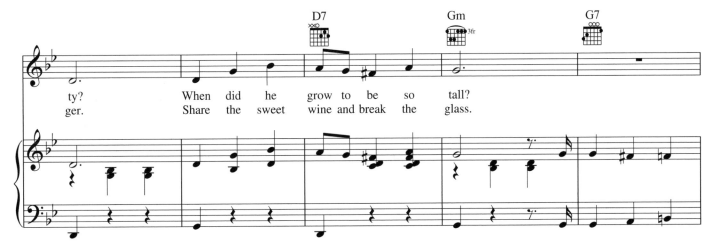

ty? When did he grow to be so tall?
ger. Share the sweet wine and break the glass.

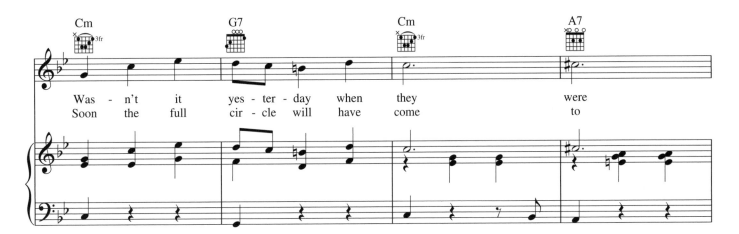

Was - n't it yes - ter - day when they were
Soon the full cir - cle will have come to

small?
pass.

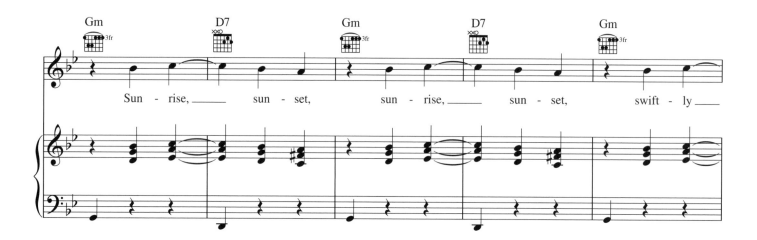

Sun - rise, _____ sun - set, sun - rise, _____ sun - set, swift - ly _____

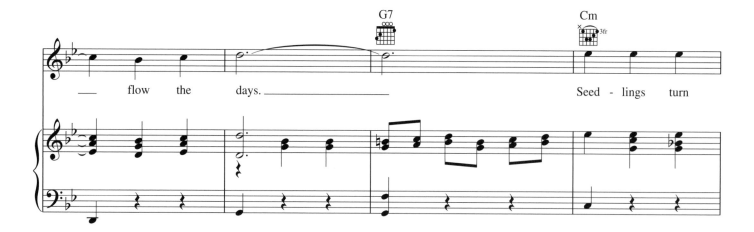

_____ flow the days. _____ Seed - lings turn

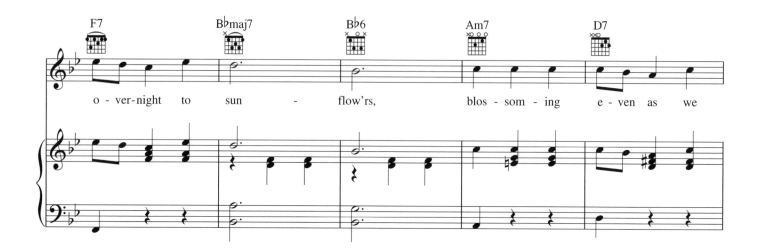

o - ver - night to sun - flow'rs, blos - som - ing e - ven as we

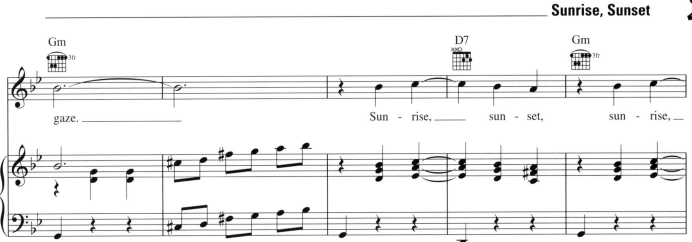

gaze. _____ Sun - rise, _____ sun - set, sun - rise, _

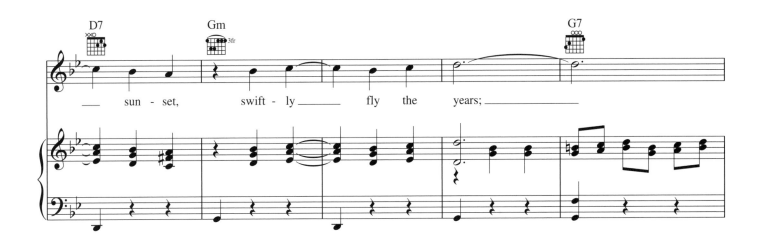

_ sun - set, swift - ly _____ fly the years; _____

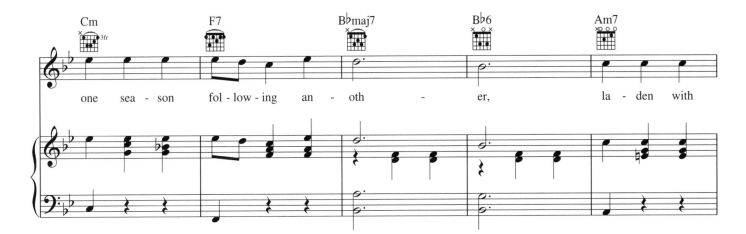

one sea - son fol - low - ing an - oth - er, la - den with

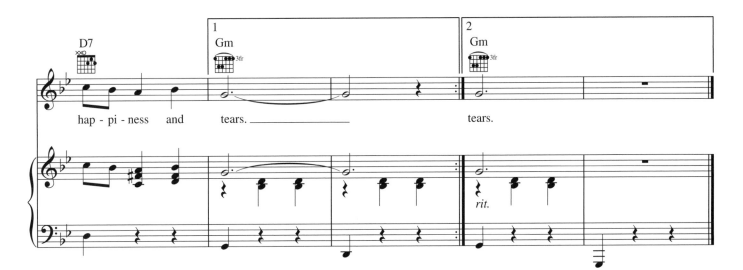

hap - pi - ness and tears. _____ tears.

The Surrey With The Fringe On Top

from OKLAHOMA!

Lyrics by Oscar Hammerstein II
Music by Richard Rodgers

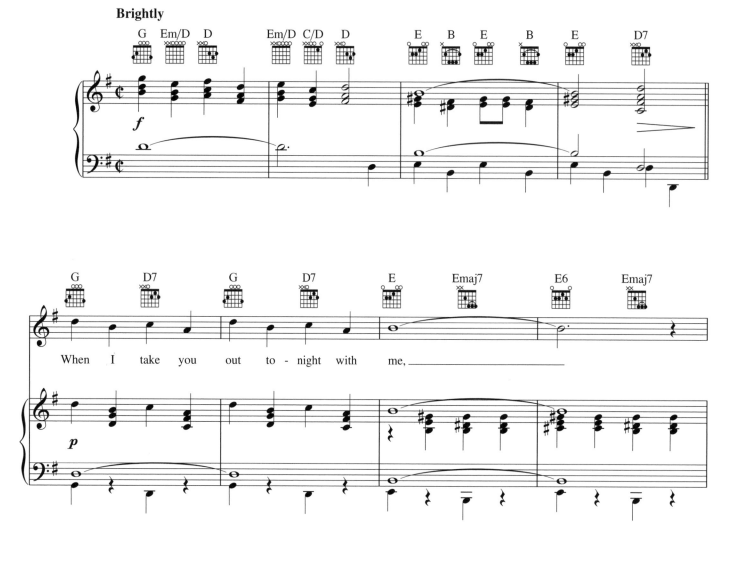

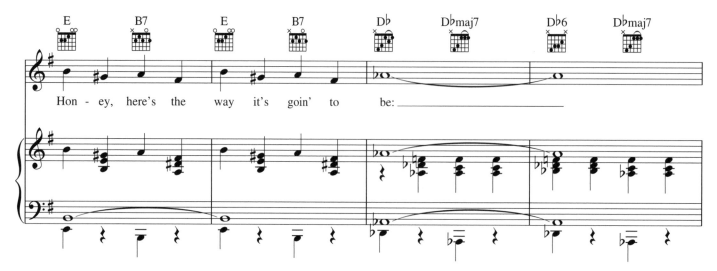

You will set be - hind a team of snow - white hors - es,

in the slick - est gig you ev - er see! ____

Refrain

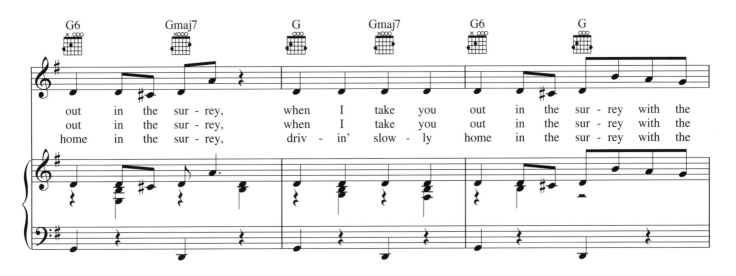

Chicks and ducks and geese bet - ter scur - ry when I take you
All the world - 'll fly in a flur - ry when I take you
I can see the stars get - tin' blur - ry when we drive back

out in the sur - rey, when I take you out in the sur - rey with the
out in the sur - rey, when I take you out in the sur - rey with the
home in the sur - rey, driv - in' slow - ly home in the sur - rey with the

fringe   on   top!   Watch   that   fringe   and   see   how   it   flut - ters

fringe   on   top!   When   we   hit   that   road,   hell   fer   leath - er,

fringe   on   top!   I   can   feel   the   day   get - tin' old - er,

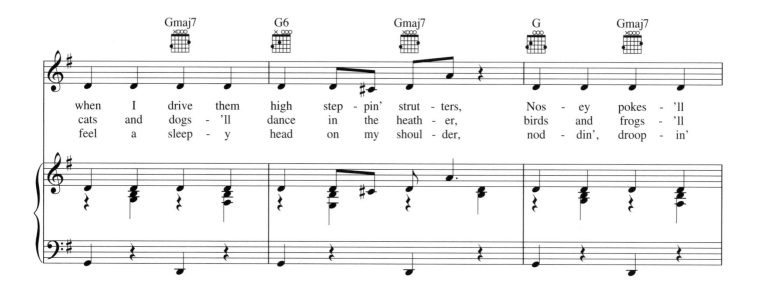

when   I   drive   them   high   step - pin'   strut - ters,   Nos - ey   pokes - 'll

cats   and   dogs - 'll   dance   in   the   heath - er,   birds   and   frogs - 'll

feel   a   sleep - y   head   on   my   shoul - der,   nod - din',   droop - in'

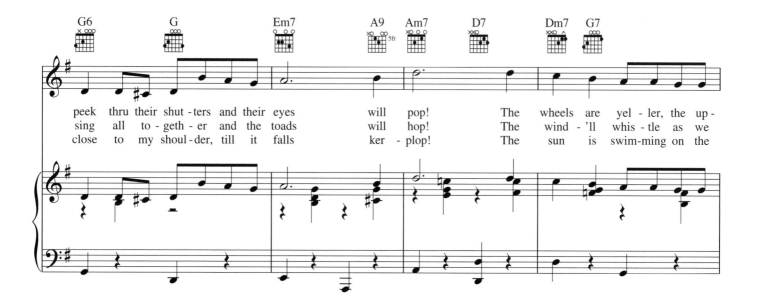

peek   thru   their   shut - ters   and   their   eyes   will   pop!   The   wheels   are   yel - ler, the up -

sing   all   to - geth - er   and   the   toads   will   hop!   The   wind - 'll   whis - tle   as   we

close   to   my   shoul - der,   till   it   falls   ker - plop!   The   sun   is   swim - ming   on   the

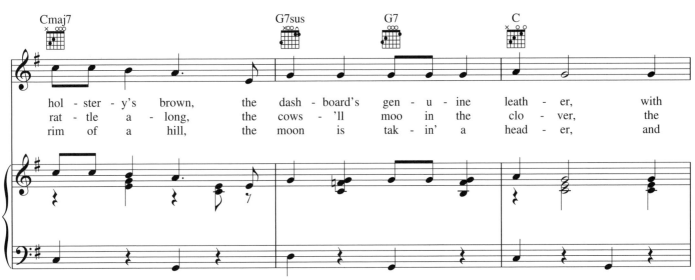

Cmaj7 · · · G7sus · G7 · C

hol -ster -y's brown, the dash -board's gen -u -ine leath -er, with
rat -tle a -long, the cows -'ll moo in the clo -ver, with the
rim of a hill, the moon is tak -in' a head -er, and

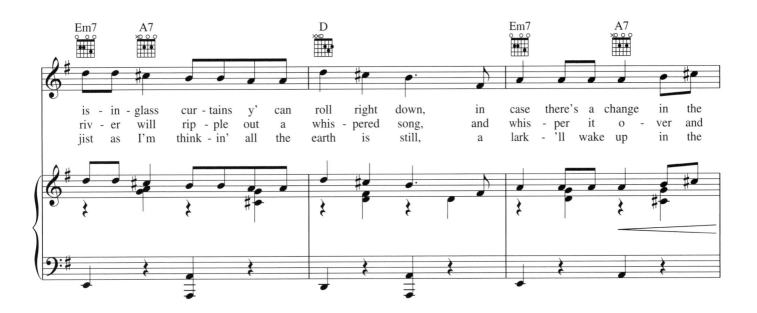

Em7 · A7 · D · Em7 · A7

is -in -glass cur -tains y' can roll right down, in case there's a change in the
riv -er will rip -ple out a whis -pered song, and whis -per it o -ver and
jist as I'm think -in' all the earth is still, a lark -'ll wake up in the

Am7/D · D7 · G · Gmaj7 · G6 · G · Gmaj7

weath -er.
o -ver: Two bright side -light's wink -in' and blink -in', ain't no fin -er
med -der. Hush, you bird, my ba -by's a -sleep -in'! May -be got a

Don't you wisht y'd go on for -ev -er? Don't you wisht y'd

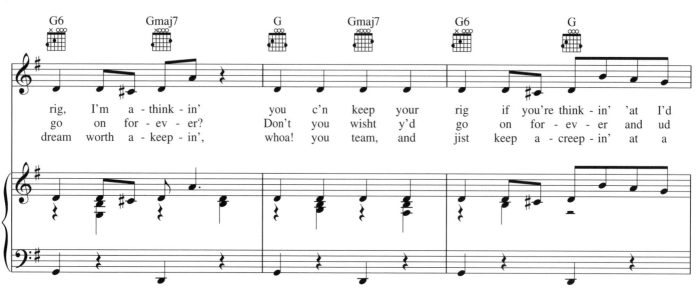

rig,   I'm a - think - in'   you   c'n   keep   your   rig if you're think - in' 'at I'd
go   on for - ev - er?   Don't you wisht y'd   go   on for - ev - er and   ud
dream worth a - keep - in',   whoa! you team, and   jist   keep a - creep - in' at   a

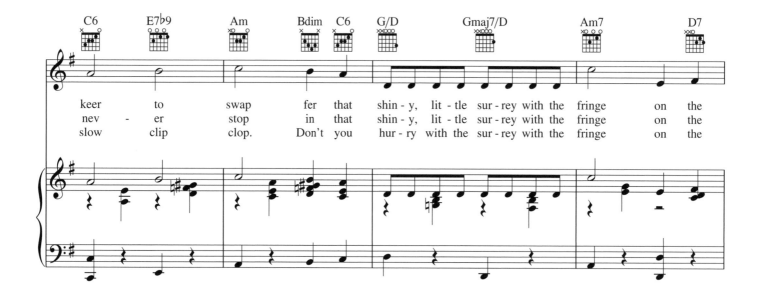

keer   to   swap   fer that   shin - y, lit - tle sur - rey with the   fringe   on   the
nev - er   stop   in that   shin - y, lit - tle sur - rey with the   fringe   on   the
slow   clip   clop.   Don't you   hur - ry with the sur - rey with the   fringe   on   the

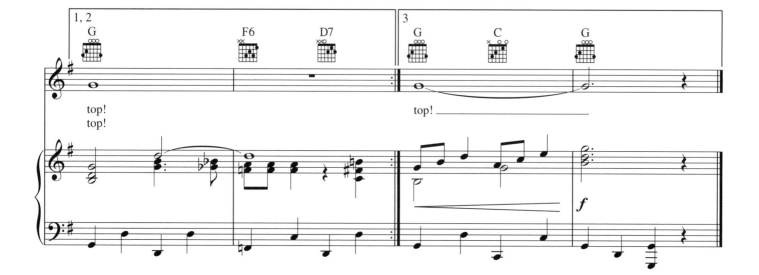

top!
top!   top!

'Til Him

from THE PRODUCERS
Music and Lyrics by Mel Brooks

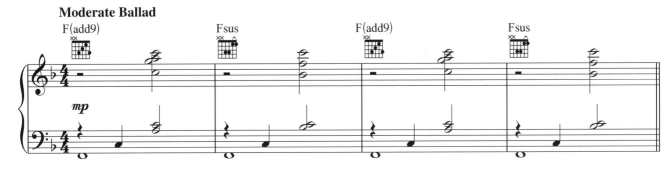

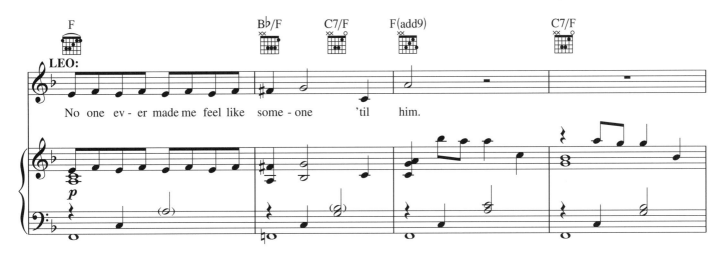

LEO: No one ev-er made me feel like some-one 'til him.

Life was real-ly noth-ing but a glum one 'til him.

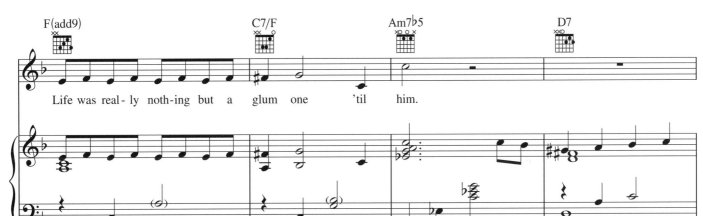

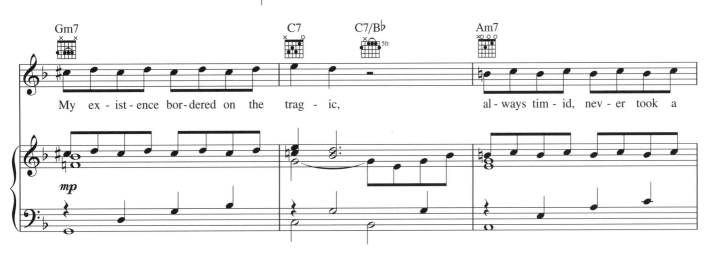

My ex-ist-ence bor-dered on the trag-ic, al-ways tim-id, nev-er took a

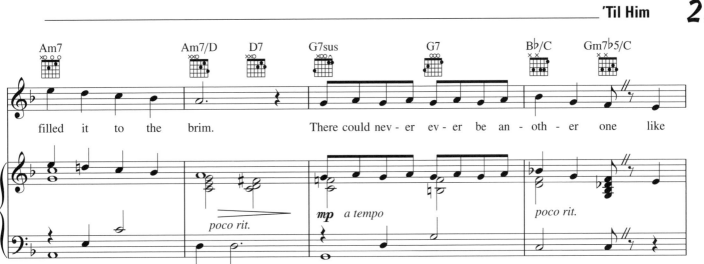

filled it to the brim. There could nev - er ev - er be an - oth - er one like

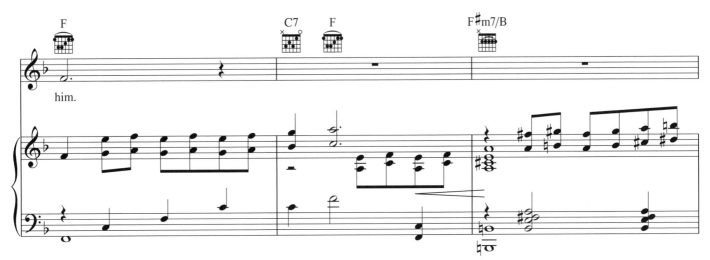

him.

MAX:

No one ev - er ev - er real - ly knew me 'til

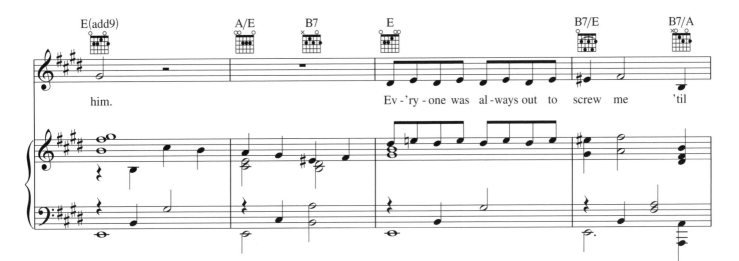

him.

Ev -'ry - one was al - ways out to screw me 'til

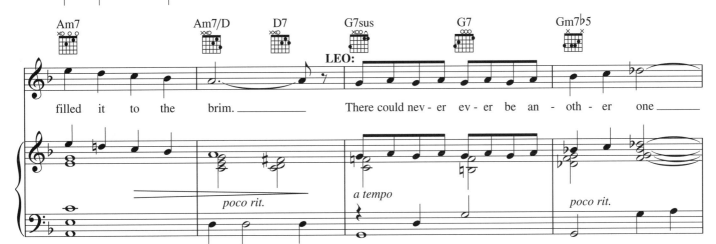

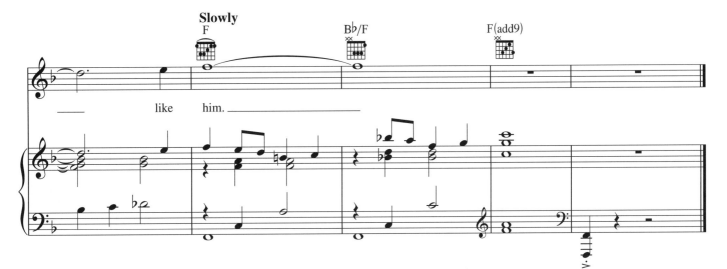

They Say It's Wonderful

from the Stage Production ANNIE GET YOUR GUN
Words and Music by Irving Berlin

Annie: Ru - mors fly and you
Frank: Ru - mors fly and you

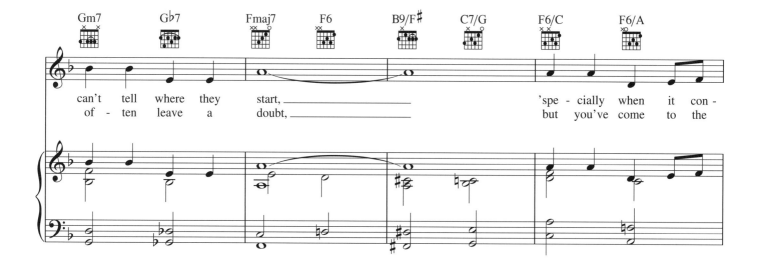

can't tell where they start, _____ 'spe - cially when it con -
of - ten leave a doubt, _____ but you've come to the

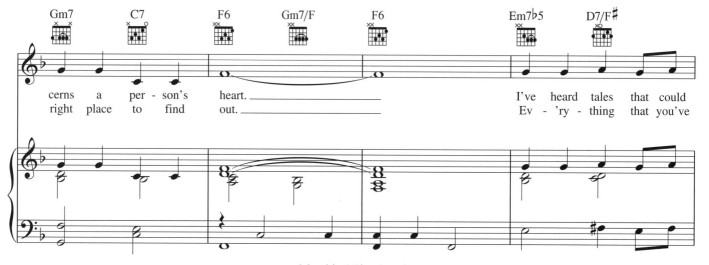

cerns a per - son's heart. _____ I've heard tales that could
right place to find out. _____ Ev - 'ry - thing that you've

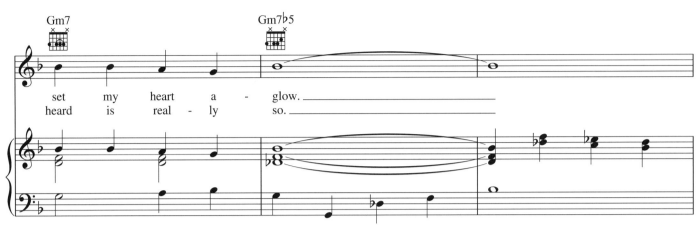

set my heart a - glow.
heard is real - ly so.

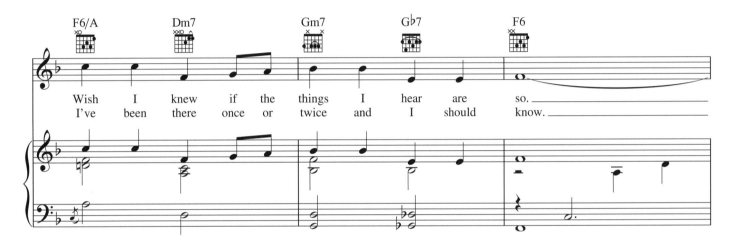

Wish I knew if the things I hear are so.
I've been there once or twice and I should know.

Slowly

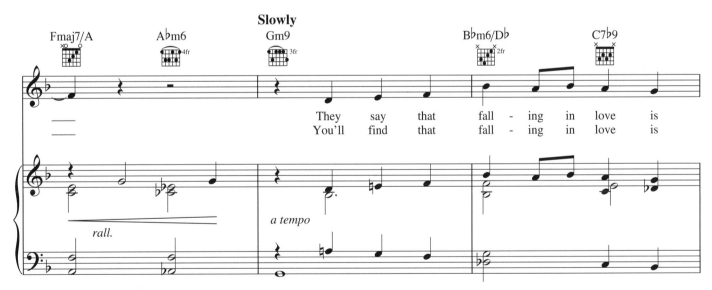

rall. *a tempo*

They say that fall - ing in love is
You'll find that fall - ing in love is

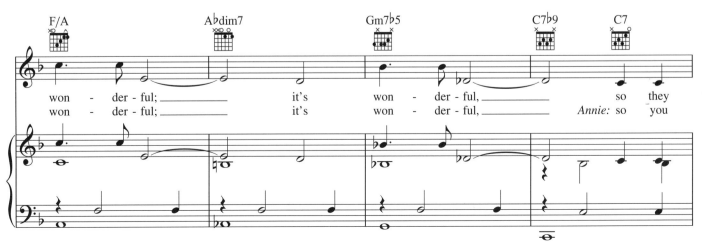

won - der - ful; it's won - der - ful, so they
won - der - ful; it's won - der - ful, *Annie:* so you

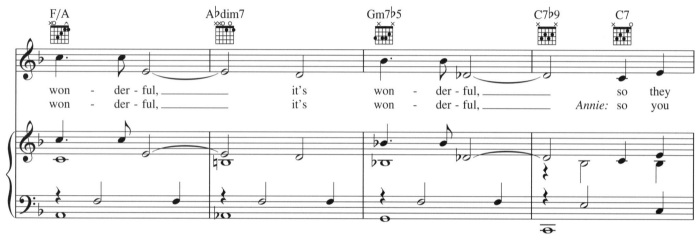

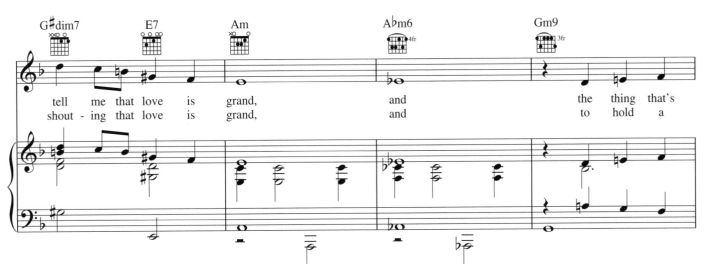

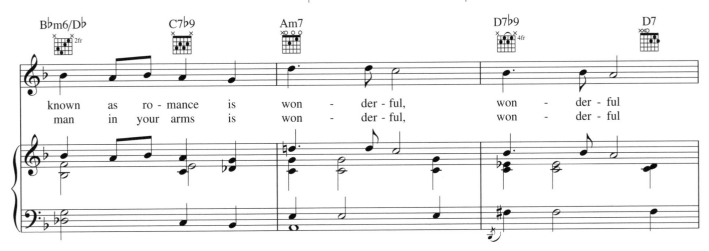

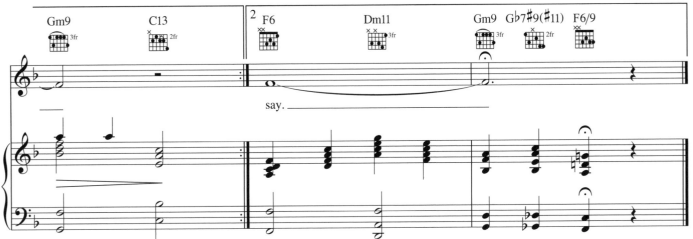

Till There Was You

from Meredith Willson's THE MUSIC MAN
By Meredith Willson

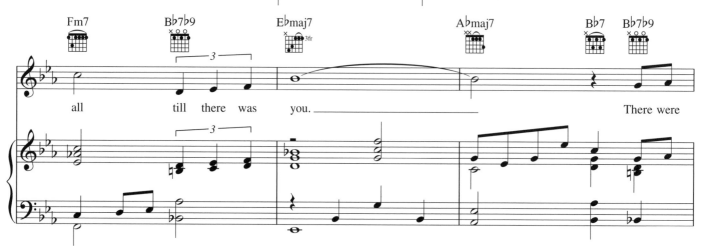

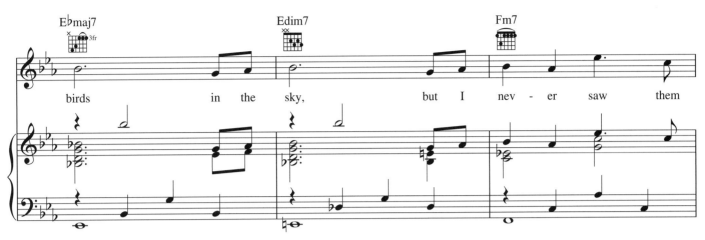

birds in the sky, but I nev-er saw them

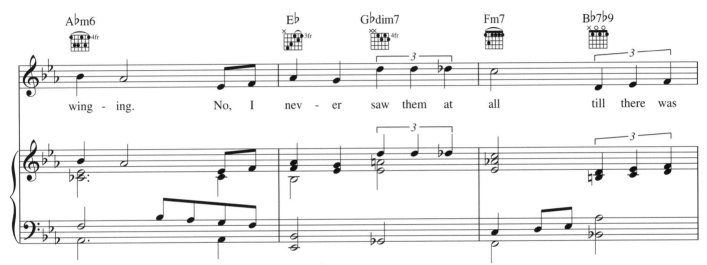

wing-ing. No, I nev-er saw them at all till there was

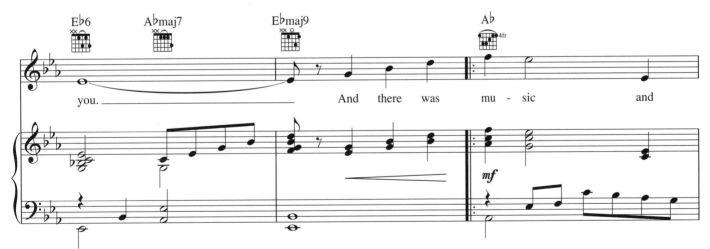

you. _____ And there was mu-sic and

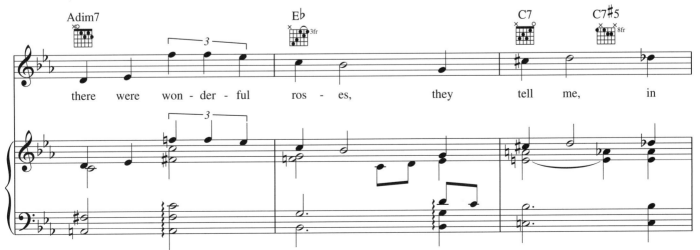

there were won-der-ful ros - es, they tell me, in

Who Can I Turn To (When Nobody Needs Me)

from THE ROAR OF THE GREASEPAINT - THE SMELL OF THE CROWD
Words and Music by Leslie Bricusse and Anthony Newley

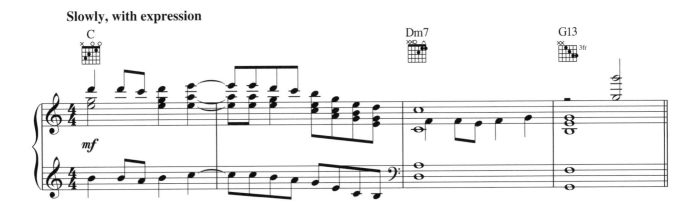

Who can I turn to _____ when no-bod-y needs me? _____ My

heart wants to know and so I must go where des-ti-ny leads me. _____

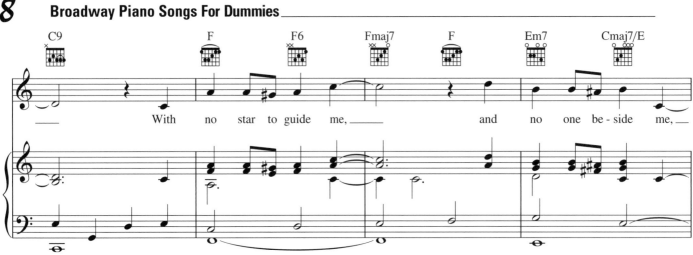

With no star to guide me, _____ and no one be - side me, _____

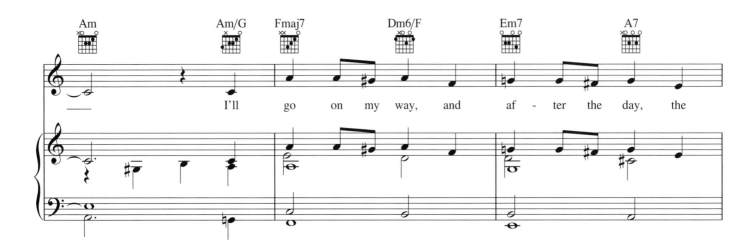

_____ I'll go on my way, and af - ter the day, the

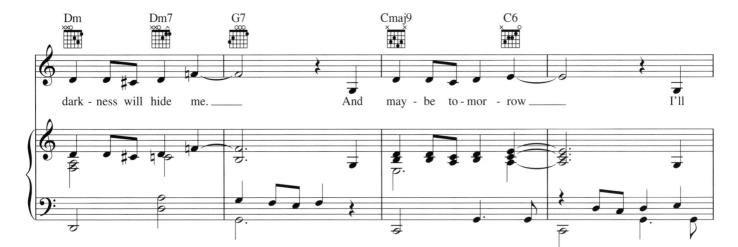

dark - ness will hide me. _____ And may - be to - mor - row _____ I'll

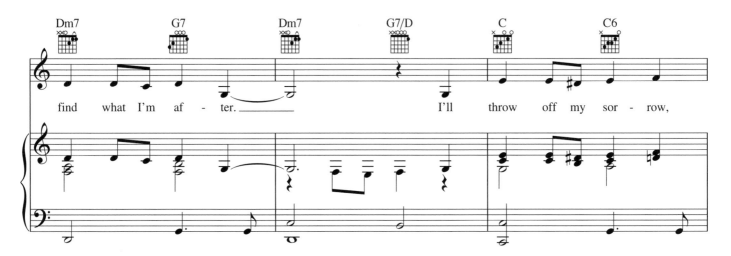

find what I'm af - ter. _____ I'll throw off my sor - row,

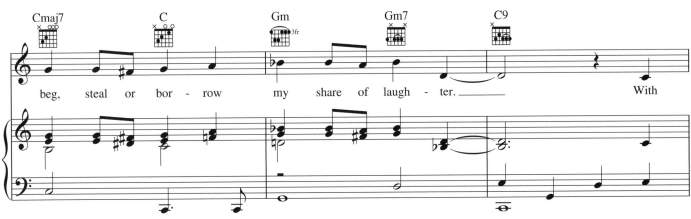

beg, steal or bor - row my share of laugh - ter. _____ With

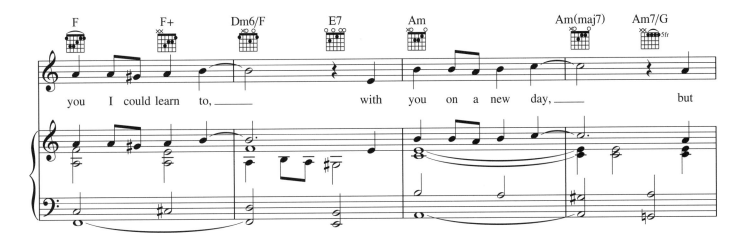

you I could learn to, _____ with you on a new day, _____ but

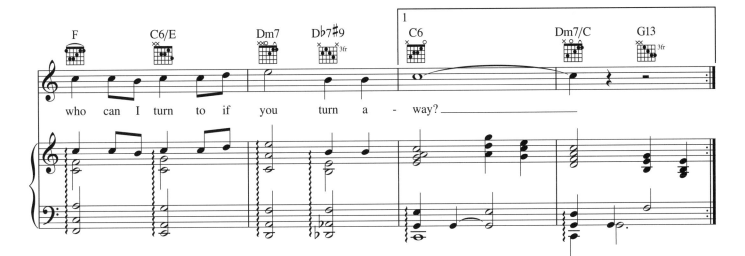

who can I turn to if you turn a - way? _____

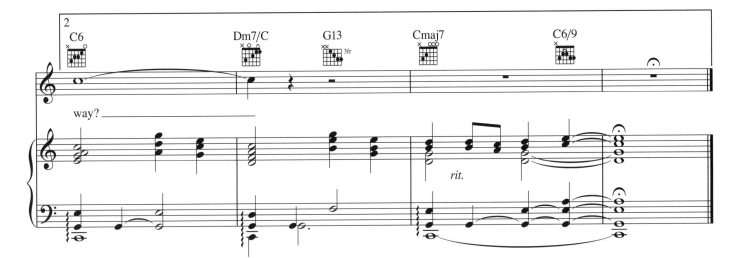

way? _____

rit.

Tomorrow

from the Musical Production ANNIE
Lyric by Martin Charnin
Music by Charles Strouse

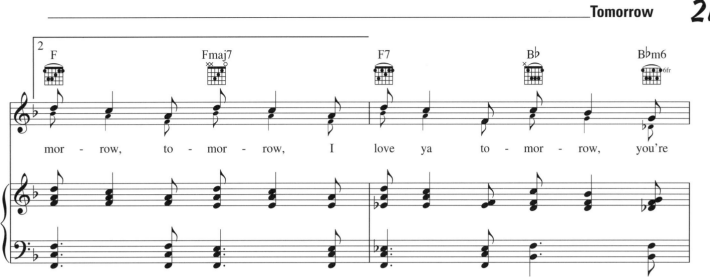

mor - row, to - mor - row, I love ya to - mor - row, you're

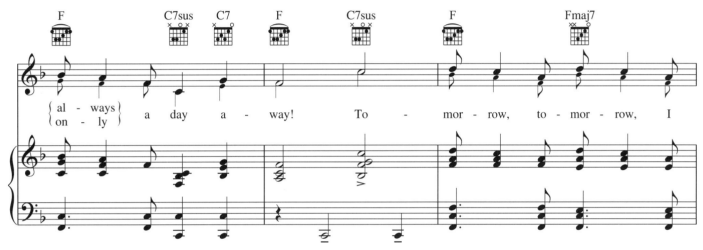

{al - ways / on - ly} a day a - way! To - mor - row, to - mor - row, I

love ya to - mor - row, you're {al - ways / on - ly} a day a -

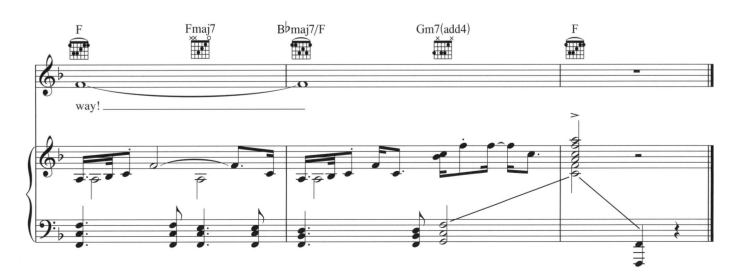

way!

What I Did For Love

from A CHORUS LINE
Music by Marvin Hamlisch
Lyric by Edward Kleban

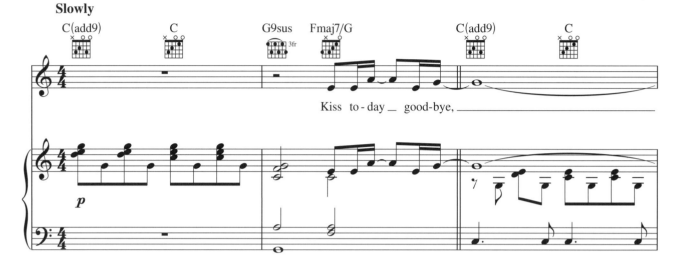

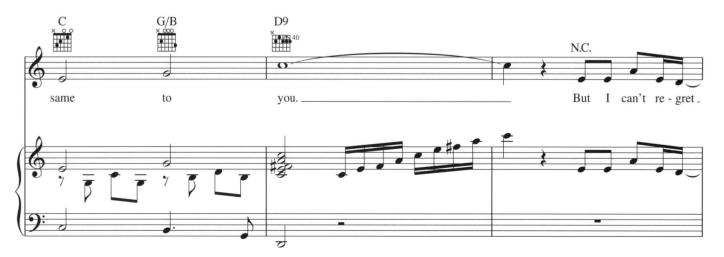

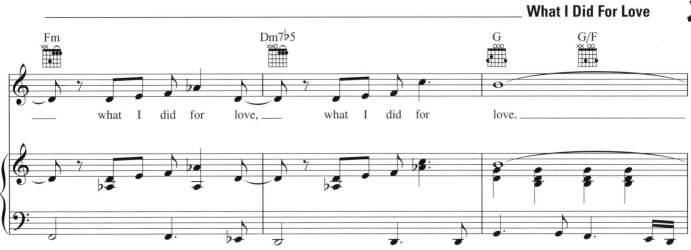

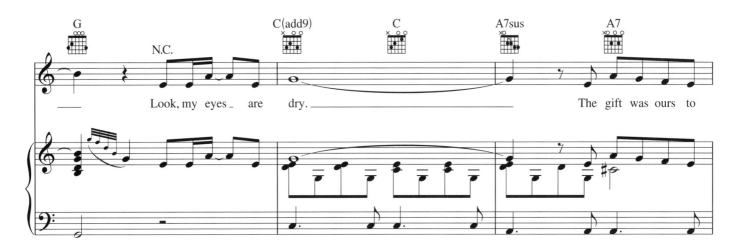

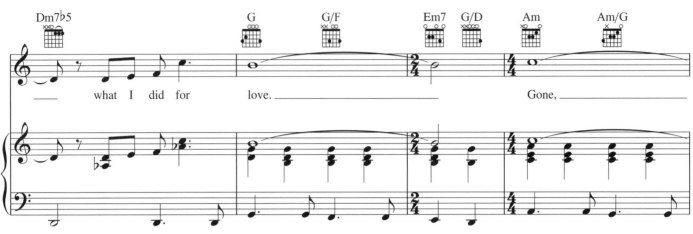

what I did for love. Gone,

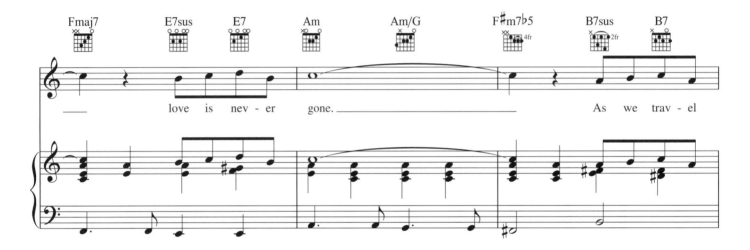

love is nev - er gone. As we trav - el

on, love's what we'll re - mem - ber.

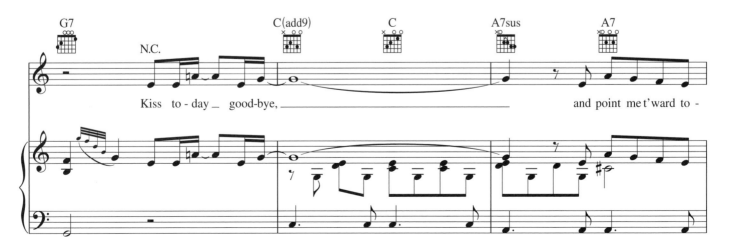

Kiss to - day good-bye, and point me t'ward to -

mor - row. _____ We did what _ we had ____ to

do. _____ Won't for - get, ____ can't re - gret _ what I did _

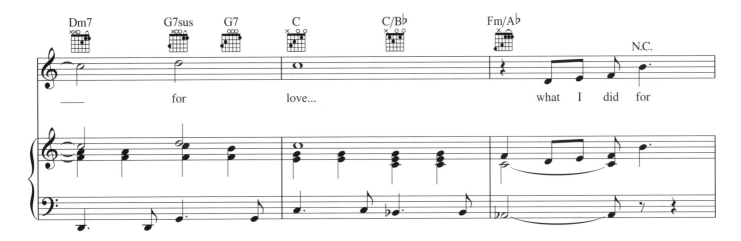

____ for love... what I did for

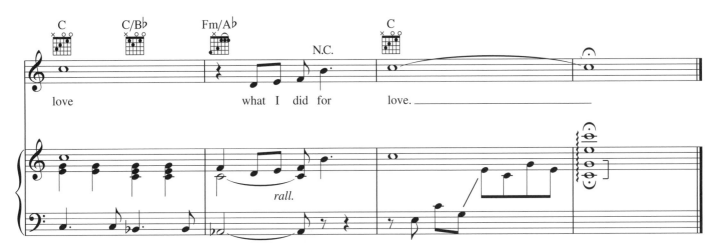

love what I did for love. _____

Younger Than Springtime

from SOUTH PACIFIC

Lyrics by Oscar Hammerstein II
Music by Richard Rodgers

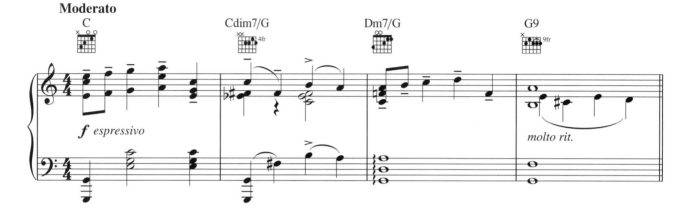

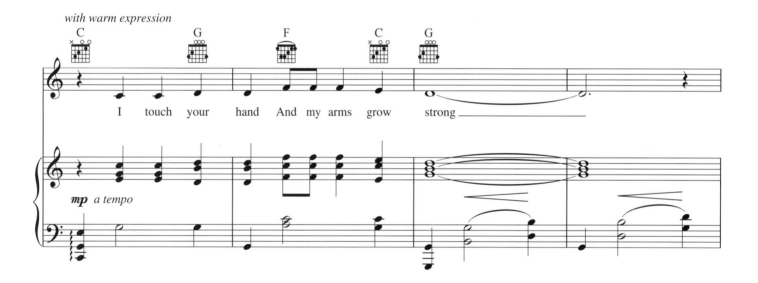

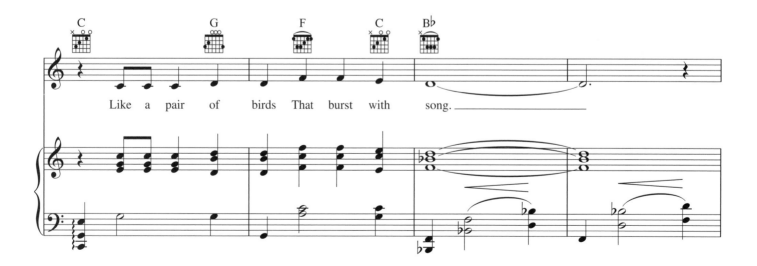

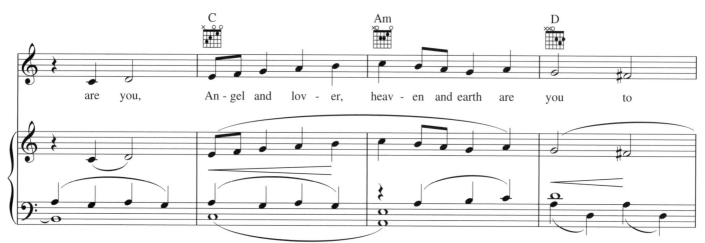

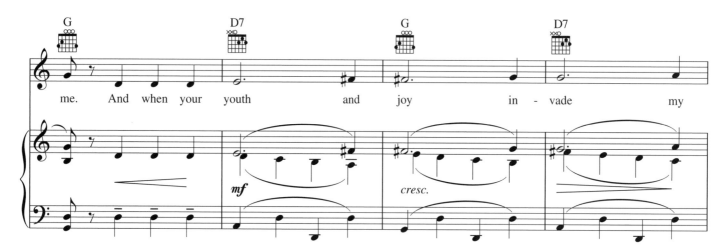

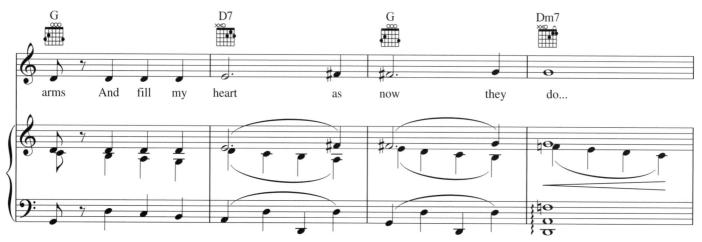

A Wonderful Day Like Today

from THE ROAR OF THE GREASEPAINT - THE SMELL OF THE CROWD
Words and Music by Leslie Bricusse and Anthony Newley

moment I woke with the lark, ___ We were both of us sing-ing a-

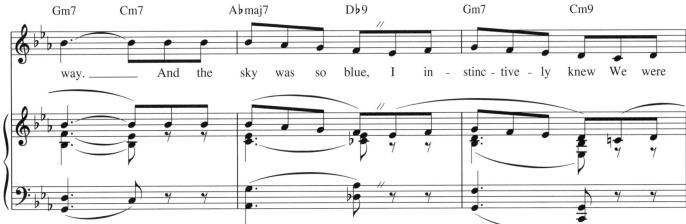

way. ___ And the sky was so blue, I in-stinc-tive-ly knew We were

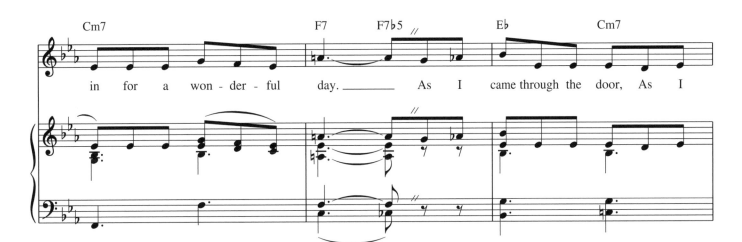

in for a won-der-ful day. ___ As I came through the door, As I

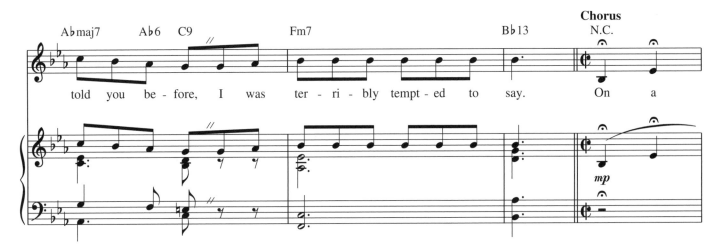

told you be-fore, I was ter-ri-bly tempt-ed to say. On a

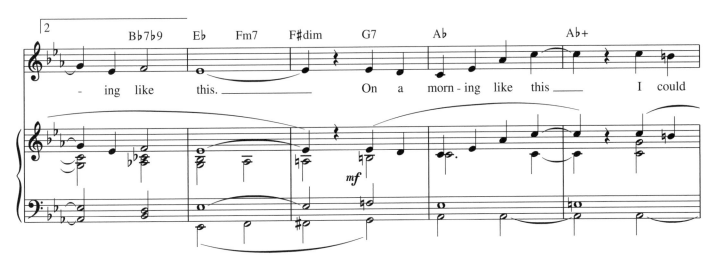

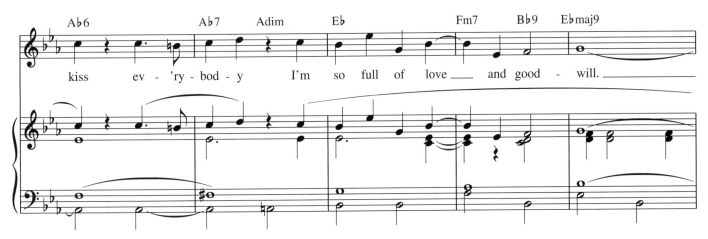

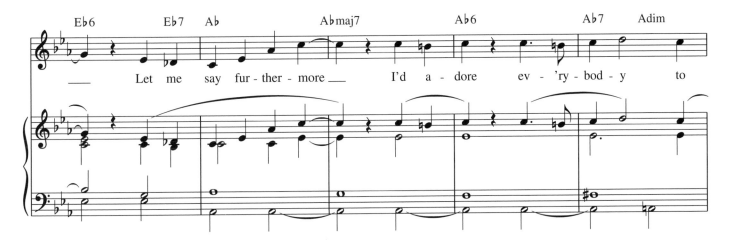

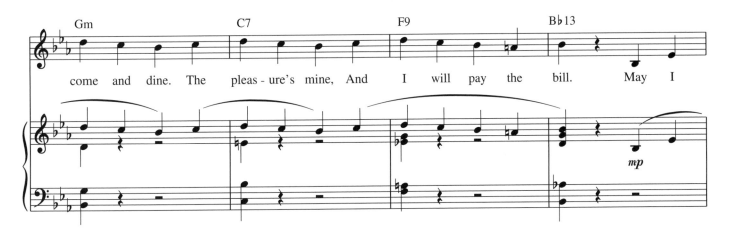

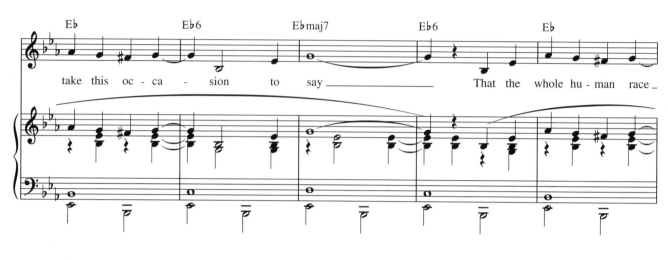

take this oc - ca - sion to say _____ That the whole hu - man race _____

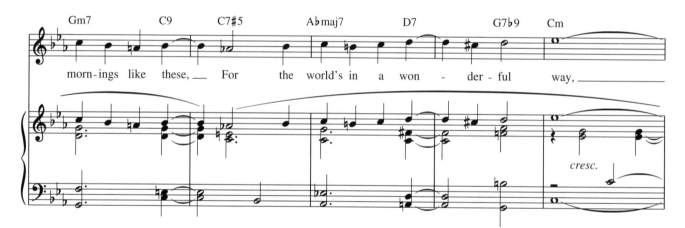

_____ should go down on its knees, _____ Show that we're grate - ful for

morn-ings like these, _____ For the world's in a won - der - ful way, _____

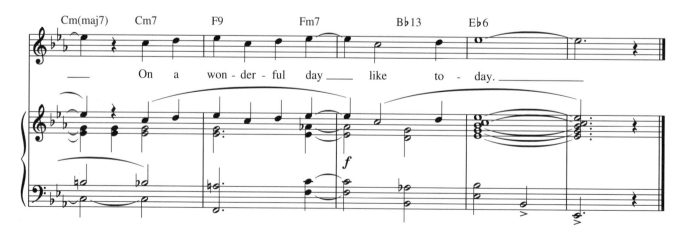

_____ On a won - der - ful day _____ like to - day. _____